C000143325

STEPS TO LIFE

STEPS TO LIFE

A SPIRITUAL JOURNEY WITH
CHRISTIAN MYSTICISM AND THE TWELVE STEPS

JOANNA THYER

ABC
Books

Published by ABC Books for the
AUSTRALIAN BROADCASTING CORPORATION
GPO Box 9994 Sydney NSW 2001

Copyright © Joanna Thyer 2004

First published July 2004

All rights reserved. No part of this publication may be reproduced, stored in a retrieval system or transmitted in any form or by any means, electronic, mechanical, photocopying, recording or otherwise, without the prior written permission of the Australian Broadcasting Corporation.

The Twelve Steps and the excerpts from *Daily Reflections*, *The Twelve Steps and Twelve Traditions*, *Alcoholics Anonymous*, and *Came to Believe* are reprinted with permission of Alcoholics Anonymous World Services Inc. (AAWS).

Permission to reprint the Twelve Steps and these excerpts does not mean that AAWS has reviewed or approved the contents of this publication, or that AAWS necessarily agrees with the views expressed herein. AA is a program of recovery from alcoholism *only* — use of the Twelve Steps and these excerpts in connection with programs and activities which are patterned after AA, but which address other problems, or in any other non-AA context, does not imply otherwise. Although Alcoholics Anonymous is a spiritual program, AA is not a religious program, and use of AA material in their present connection does not imply AA's affiliation with, or endorsement of, any sect, denomination or specific religious belief.

ISBN 0 7333 1417 1

Cover photograph by Shaun Egan/Getty Images
Designed by Christabella Designs
Set in Sabon 11/18 by Christabella Designs
Colour reproduction by Colorwize Studio, Adelaide
Printed and bound in Australia by Griffin Press, Adelaide

5 4 3 2 1

ACKNOWLEDGMENTS

I am particularly grateful to Alcoholics Anonymous and The AA Grapevine for allowing me to liberally use their material. I hope I have given it the respect it deserves.

I would especially like to thank Father Steve Sinn SJ and Father Brian Stoney for their feedback, guidance and support with this book, particularly with the references to St Ignatius. I would also like to thank Brother Dominic Brogan for his expertise on Christian Spirituality; Michael McGirr; Alan Sharpe (may he rest in peace) for his editorial wisdom and encouragement in my early days as a writer; writer Debi Marshall for her refreshing insight; Diane Young and Kate Brake for their discerning eye and input. Special thanks goes to my mother Josephine for her constant help with the editing of the manuscript.

Thanks to all my friends for their support, particularly those friends and acquaintances who have allowed me to use their stories for this book.

I apologise for all the times I have failed to use inclusive language in this book. Since most of the texts are very old, and many of the Twelve Step texts were written in the first half of the twentieth century, it is difficult to maintain consistent attention to inclusiveness. I hope a spirit of inclusiveness comes through.

AUTHOR'S NOTE

My approach has been a holistic one – the mental, emotional and spiritual aspects of a person's being need to be addressed on any spiritual journey. The aim is to use the best and most helpful aspects of the Christian spiritual tradition, and combine them with the Twelve Step program. It is about a spiritual process that begins with admission of personal powerlessness, which grows with continual acceptance of that fact, and which gives birth to an undreamed of capacity for greater personal freedom and intimacy with God.

Steps to Life is meant purely for reflection and for anyone interested in enhancing their spiritual development. It is not meant as a 'this is how it ought to be done' book for those in Twelve Step recovery programs. While the Twelve Step program can be used by anyone interested in spiritual growth, *Steps to Life* may be of particular interest to those who have dealt with their addictions and want to deepen their spiritual life, as well as anyone who has experienced life crises, such as breakdowns, relationship break-ups and so on, and wants to be able to grow through them.

I have included quotes and personal stories with each chapter to make the nature of the spiritual journey more accessible. It is through our stories that we remain connected to each other and to God.

Joanna Thyer, 2004

CONTENTS

EPIGRAPH

Midway this way of life we're bound upon,
I woke to find myself in a dark wood,
Where the right road was wholly lost and gone.

Ay me! How hard to speak of it — that rude
And rough and stubborn forest! The mere breath
Of memory stirs the old fear in the blood;

It is so bitter, it goes nigh to death;
Yet there I gained such good, that, to convey
The tale, I'll write what else I found therewith.

Dante's The Divine Comedy.[1]

INTRODUCTION
THE DESIRE FOR CONNECTION

*The call today is to transcend this world of signs
and symbols, and enter the new creation, the new
world which is revealed in all the great traditions.
This is the call of humanity today.
We are all involved in it.*
(Bede Griffiths)[1]

HOW THE TWELVE STEPS BEGAN

On any night in any city in the world, people from all walks of life, of every sex, race and religion gather in halls or community centres to meet with those who call themselves 'anonymous'. These Twelve Step groups might be made up of gamblers, alcoholics, drug addicts or any other group of people seeking recovery from an addiction.

It is no coincidence and no mean feat that the spiritual movement of the Twelve Steps, which began in the 1930s, was conceived when two men both suffering the same problem of addiction got together to help each other. From such small beginnings millions of lives have been transformed.

This movement, which became the AA (Alcoholics Anonymous) program, gained many of its ideas from the Oxford Group, a spiritual movement which had its beginnings in 1908 when Frank Buchman, a passionate and ambitious Lutheran pastor from Philadelphia, USA, experienced a life-changing spiritual transformation while attending a religious convention in Keswick, England. After experiencing a profound sense of spiritual separateness, Buchman became overwhelmed with the desire to completely surrender to God. This prompted him to make amends to committee members he had argued with on a settlement house project, a hospice for the poor, back in Philadelphia. He wrote to each person: 'Am writing to tell you that I have harboured an unkind feeling toward you — at times I conquered it but it always came back. Our views may differ but as brothers we must love. I write to ask your forgiveness and to assure you that I love you and trust by God's grace I shall never more speak unkindly or disparagingly of you.'[2] Each time he wrote a letter, Buchman said he felt it in a new way, 'the last line cost me most of all, I almost wrote it in my own blood'. Eager to share this experience, he began an evangelical group at the nearby Oxford University and what became known as the Oxford Group later spread throughout the world.

The Oxford Group is extremely significant as a spiritual movement in the world, since it can be seen as the beginning of the self-help movement. The movement encouraged people to share their own spiritual journeys and reflect on their inner life, quite a radical thing at a time when the world was dramatically changing. The moral relativism of communism was growing in popularity and what was perceived to be the moral order was fading away. In light of Hitler's rise to power in the 1930s it is no surprise that the Oxford Group became known as 'moral rearmament'.

The Oxford Group based its support network on 'the four absolutes' — love, honesty, purity, unselfishness — and contained many elements of the Christian spiritual tradition that were free of the traditional dogma associated with the churches. Like AA, the Oxford Group also involved individuals sharing their different stories. Looking back on this significant history, one of AA's founders, Bill W, would later describe the Oxford Group as 'a non-denominational evangelical movement streamlined for the modern world'.[3]

One might say that the seeds of the Twelve Step experience were sown when the famous Swiss psychoanalyst Carl Jung met with Rowland H, an alcoholic who was desperately trying to get sober. Jung informed him that in his experience only those who experienced a major psychic change or a dramatic spiritual awakening, leading to 'huge emotional displacements and rearrangements', were able to get sober.

Rowland adamantly responded to this, saying that he was a man of faith. Jung retorted with strong sentiments. He knew the severity of the problem, 'ordinary religious faith isn't enough ...' a 'transforming experience, a conversion experience' is needed '... recognise your personal hopelessness ... cast yourself upon whatever God you think there is ...'[4]

Following this, Rowland attended the Oxford Group that, in essence, had the following teachings:

1. Admit powerlessness in managing one's life.

2. Become honest with self; make an examination of conscience.

3. Make a rigorous confession of personal defects in order to not be alone with problems.

4. Look at distorted relationships and make amends to people wherever possible.

5. Resolve to help others in need without seeking prestige or material gain.

6. Through meditation seek God's direction and help and try to practice these principles of conduct always.[5]

BILL W

Before the coming of faith I had lived as an alien in
a cosmos that too often seemed both hostile and
cruel. In it there could be no inner security for me.
(Bill W)[6]

In December 1934 in Towns Hospital, New York, Bill W, a chronic alcoholic, lay in a hospital bed after yet another drinking binge, overcome by the blackest depression he had ever known. This blackness was followed by a spiritual experience that changed his life forever — a 'white light' experience of Spirit, that overwhelmed and liberated him.

On hearing about Bill's spiritual conversion, Bill's doctor, Dr Silkworth, wisely discerned that Bill had undergone a psychic experience, which could help him with his problem. He reassured him he had not gone mad.

Just before his conversion experience, Bill had been visited by his friend Ebby, who had become an Oxford Group member via his friend Rowland H, and who gently told him his formula for recovery. Ebby also gave Bill a book, William James' *Varieties of Religious Experience*, which explained that the conversion experience had an objective reality: it could alter motivation.

Several months after his Towns Hospital experience Bill had an overwhelming desire to drink one night. As fate would have it, he was introduced to Dr Bob S, an Akron surgeon and alcoholic. Over long discussions into the night, they came to an understanding that by synthesising medical knowledge and spirituality with the individual alcoholic's experience, sobriety was possible.[7] In other words, by combining a holistic mental, physical and spiritual approach to the treatment of alcoholism and seeing it as a disease, a person could begin the road to recovery and also gain a new lease of life.

These early experiences of Bill and Bob served to be the genesis of what some have called the greatest spiritual movement of the twentieth century. Both men set up groups in their respective cities and slowly the society of Alcoholics Anonymous was born. The word-of-mouth program Ebby had given Bill developed into the Twelve Steps for recovery:

1. We admitted we were powerless over alcohol — that our lives had become unmanageable.

2. Came to believe that a Power greater than ourselves could restore us to sanity.

3. Made a decision to hand our will and our lives over to the care of God as we understood him.

4. Made a searching and fearless moral inventory of ourselves.

5. Admitted to God, to ourselves and to another human being the exact nature of our wrongs.

6. Were entirely ready to have God remove all these defects of character.

7. Humbly asked Him to remove our shortcomings.

8. Made a list of all persons we had harmed, and became willing to make amends to them all.

9. Made direct amends to such people wherever possible, except when to do so would injure them or others.

10. Continued to take personal inventory and when we were wrong promptly admitted it.

11. Sought through prayer and meditation to improve our conscious contact with God, as we understood Him, praying only for knowledge of His will for us and the power to carry that out.

12. Having had a spiritual awakening as the result of these steps, we tried to carry this message to alcoholics and to practice these principles in all our affairs.[8]

Eventually this fellowship withdrew from the Oxford Group and adopted the name Alcoholics Anonymous. By 1939, the book *Alcoholics Anonymous: The Big Book* was published. In 1989 the number of books distributed had passed the eight million mark.[9] It is far greater now.

OUR INBORN DESIRE FOR GOD

The desire to transcend what you are is something unique to the human condition. It is the desire for connection with the 'Other'. It is a yearning to be home, to see the face of God, to experience hope in the mystery of life and to complete our humanity. Whether you are conscious of it or not, we all have an inborn desire for God which gives us meaning and is our deepest longing. In other words, 'wherever your treasure is, there will your heart be too' (Matthew 6:21).[10]

As the unwitting contributor to the early ideas which led to the formation of AA, Jung wrote in his memoir: 'My life is a story of the self-realisation of the unconscious ...' He wisely added: 'We are a psychic process we do not control'.[11]

The big picture of your life is up to God, and even the details are unknown to you. You are part of a much wider process.

According to Jung, 'the power of individuation' is a spiritual force, which is God's life or spirit, coming from the depth of our essential being. In essence it is our homesickness for God. In a letter to Bill W, Jung wrote that Rowland's 'craving for alcohol was the equivalent, on a low level, of the spiritual thirst for wholeness, expressed in medieval language: the union with God.' Jung added that the only right way to formulate such an experience so that it is not misunderstood in contemporary society:

... is that it happens to you in reality and it can only happen to you when you walk on a path which leads you to higher understanding. You might be led to that goal by an act of grace, or through a personal and honest contact with friends, or through a higher education of the mind beyond the confines of mere rationalism. I see from your letter that Rowland H has chosen the second way, which was, under the circumstances, obviously the best one.[12]

The quest for truth has always been part of human yearning. In the spiritual life, the search for truth can lead to an experience of a power outside oneself, sometimes experienced as 'Spirit'. As Bill W's story is testimony to, revelation and new insight are often the beginning of the discovery of such truth. 'The truth will set you free' (John 8:32) becomes a possibility when a person embarks on the Twelve Step program.

A pertinent idea for those seeking insight from Twelve Step programs is that when someone is ready to let go of their ego, especially the desire to control (often inspired by the fear of what might happen if they fall apart), they can make this connection and go beyond themselves. A commitment to be open to the Spirit or a power greater than ourselves gives us the potential and courage to face the reality of our true selves, without denial, and to confront the depths of our flawed humanity.

THE TWELVE STEPS:
A PILGRIMAGE OF THE HEART

The concept of 'pilgrimage' is part of the Christian spiritual tradition. Throughout history, Christians went on journeys or pilgrimages to holy places, thinking of them as a long trip towards heaven, their 'native land'. To incorporate the Twelve Steps into your life means to abandon yourself to a spiritual journey and to find your own 'native land', which is inevitably a pilgrimage of the heart. To do this you must be prepared to face the fear and abandonment felt on such a journey, and learn to grow in the face of feeling inspired and desolate by putting yourself at the Spirit's disposal and handing over your will and life to the Other. Benedictine writer Demetrius Dumm describes this process: 'The Spirit gives us a sense of confidence now, but at the same time, a deep feeling of homesickness as we yearn for what is still to be realised ... the full gift in the kingdom'.[13]

Through its development of the Twelve Steps, Alcoholics Anonymous unwittingly tapped into something profound in people's psyche, something about our essence as human beings and the very nature of our spiritual strivings. By emphasising that alcoholism is a threefold illness — spiritual, mental, physical — it tapped deep into the need for a holistic approach for solving the malaise of our internal angst. Addiction is not a moral problem, but a sickness that invades every aspect of a person's being. By emphasising belief in a God of your own understanding, AA also freed people from the constraints of religious dogma.

The role of Twelve Step programs in the spiritual lives of millions of people is timely as we face the complexities of living in the twenty-first century. No longer do the spiritual needs of many people fit the dualistic framework of traditional religious models. We live in a world that moves fast and constant change is the one certainty. Lack of ritual, the lack of sense of the sacred and the general lack of meaning have led many people to hunger for spirituality. Depression, suicide and other problems are partly the by-products of this lack of connection.

Today we face many grey areas: ambiguities and uncertainties in work; relationships; the financial world; and institutional structures. Many of the old institutional structures in society, including mainstream religions, are changing and in some cases disintegrating. Balancing the competing forces of postmodern life is a challenge for everyone.

The Twelve Steps offer enormous hope amid this complexity in our lives. Not only do they provide a new focus for humanity's quest for self-fulfilment and meaning, but they fuel a revitalised form of spirituality, free of some of the dogmatic constraints of religion, yet able to coincide with the essence of the Gospel, and the best that Christianity has to offer. This program can work independently for both believers and non-believers in God, or hand in hand with all the great religious traditions.

The lack of connection, the feeling of being detached from others, and from ourselves is part of the human condition, and the Twelve Steps, when integrated with essential elements of the Christian spiritual tradition, can help answer this need. Not only can they be used as a potential panacea for those with addictions, they can also provide a blueprint for spiritual development.

The ancient Greeks, such as Heraclitus, spoke of the overarching unity in the universe, the 'logos'. In the prologue of John's Gospel in the New Testament, this is indirectly referred to as 'the Word' ('In the beginning was the Word, the Word was with God and the Word was God' (John 1:1)). Reconnecting with and experiencing this unity helps us to find meaning and liberation in our universe and in our lives.

MYSTICS

There are many different definitions of what constitutes a 'mystic'. Mystics might be defined as those who experience God or the divine outside the realm of rational or temporal understanding and beyond the understanding of their own religion. They are also those who seek union with God, who, 'penetrated with the divine substance', lose themselves, or those who 'desire to know, only that they may love'. Mystics, above all, desire 'union with the principle of things in God ...'[14] Mystical states, while invariably transient, usually result in great insights into truth that cannot be intellectually comprehended.[15] Such definitions are endless. *Steps to Life* looks at some of the great Christian mystics, including the Eastern Desert Fathers of third–century monasticism, St Antony, and mystics who emerged much later, such as St John of the Cross in the sixteenth century, Julian of Norwich in the fourteenth century and the thirteenth–century Mechthild of Magdeburg. The humble St Francis of Assisi and the astute St Ignatius of Loyola may well be among those whose spirituality particularly influenced the formation of the Twelve Steps.

It is important to mention that throughout the history of the Christian tradition, the quest for perfection, originally a Hellenist (Greek) idea adopted by the Church Fathers, remained paramount. Despite this history this quest is not integral to a relationship with God. The Twelve Steps are not about achieving perfection, but about striving for authenticity. This is a crucial point in the field of spirituality. As the AA *Big Book* outlines, 'We are not saints. The point is that we are willing to grow along spiritual lines.'[16]

CHAPTER ONE:
MOMENTS OF TRUTH

Step One: We admitted we were powerless over alcohol, that our lives had become unmanageable.

'Lying there in conflict, I dropped into the blackest depression I had ever known ... I cried out, 'Now I'm ready to do anything...'
(Bill W telling his story of spiritual conversion and the journey to sobriety.)[1]

MATTHEW TALBOT'S STORY

It was outside a bar on a Saturday morning in Dublin 1884 when the 28-year-old Matt was blessed with a conversion experience, which ultimately led to him receiving the grace to abstain from alcohol for the rest of his life.

Broke and dejected after his drinking friends refused him drinking money, he stood draped around a lamp post for a while, then walked towards a canal. It was there that he underwent a strange conversion experience, a flash of insight, where he suddenly saw himself as he really was: rejected, penniless, self-centred, mean, a slave to alcohol.

Later that afternoon he went to confession where he promised to abstain from alcohol for three months. His confessor was wise to the fact that Matt would need special help to remain sober and encouraged him in his decision to go to daily Mass and Holy Communion, something not even expected of the devoutly religious in those days. Matt went through agonising alcohol withdrawal on his own as these were the days before AA or detoxes. Under the guidance of a Jesuit spiritual director he adopted an austere routine of prayer, fasting and theological education.

In 1890 he made another pledge to seek Christian perfection and joined the Third Order of St Francis. Matt's spiritual advisors chose a strict Rule of the early Irish monasteries: prayer, penance, fasting, work and study.[2] In this Matt was not unlike the early monastics in the way he went about his spiritual devotion. He also managed to stay sober for the rest of his life. Perhaps what marks Matt Talbot's spiritual journey was his openness to where the Spirit was leading him and his willingness to go to any lengths.

HOW THE JOURNEY BEGINS: ABANDONMENT AND PILGRIMAGE

Like Matt Talbot, to admit complete defeat in any area of life is to let go of the ties that bind. It can occur at any time in life for all kinds of reasons. The feelings of disintegration, despair, loneliness, emptiness, alienation, abandonment and separation are often the symptoms of a crisis leading to a turning point where you see yourself as you really are. It might be addiction that has led you to this point or it might be depression or a breakdown or a similar shattering life experience. Whatever the causes and events leading up to you taking this step, the invariable outcome is 'do or die'.

Ironically, when you come to a point where you accept

you are beaten and broken, you become liberated. As Benedictine writer Demetrius Dumm says, 'Bondage alone leads to nothing; bondage acknowledged opens the way to salvation'.[3]

When Bill W cried out in Towns Hospital, 'I am ready to do anything', he was in effect taking Step One in admitting his complete powerlessness and helplessness in the face of his addiction, in the face of his very humanity. Step One is about coming to a turning point where you admit you are completely powerless, where you have totally given in. It is saying to your conscious self, 'I am totally beaten, I cannot fight this on my own'.

It is also saying 'my life is chaos'. This may involve giving in to the chaos. It may have taken a nervous breakdown, a suicide attempt or a similar rock bottom situation to come to that point. Deep within you are standing on the verge of a complete rearrangement of your essential self. As Jung stressed to Roland H, emotional rearrangements and displacements are taking place. You enter into a new way of being.

Just as they were for Matt Talbot and Bill W, moments of truth can often be 'saving' events for people. When you take Step One the event that has moved you to this is 'saving' because it frees you from the bondage of denial and all the emotional energy needed to maintain that facade.

To admit powerlessness over something is the beginning of experiencing freedom. It is a spiritual experience, since so much of living a spiritual life is about becoming free to be who you really are. It is the beginning of the journey of becoming free of the bondage of self.

You become a new person when you take Step One. Not only do you suddenly see yourself as you really are, but you also discover who you really are. You are beginning to self-integrate and undergo a self-actualisation process where there is increased awareness, freedom, relatedness and a sense of going beyond yourself.[4]

DEATH AND RESURRECTION: DYING TO THE OLD WAYS OF LIVING

Often faith stories involve a 'death' and a 'resurrection'. At various times in our lives we are faced with crises that can only be worked through by 'dying' to our old way of living. These moments of truth where you accept you are beaten or broken are all part of a death–rebirth cycle, a never-ending spiritual process. A 'death' of self is experienced in order to 'live'. 'Death' can mean loss of spiritual life, loss of meaning or loss of any sense of identity. There is no choice in these situations. You have reached a crossroads.

Such breakdowns coming from forms of addiction such as alcoholism, crises, or from what medieval mystic St John of the Cross called, 'the long dark night of the soul', can ultimately bring you to a state of spiritual rebirth and this can be revelatory. These tragic experiences not only open you up for God to come into your life, but they also pave the way for you to be introduced to yourself, 'to grow along spiritual lines'[5] in a way that you cannot anticipate. The author Victor Frankl writing of his experiences in a Nazi concentration camp sums this up as, 'suffering introduces me to myself.'[6]

THE BACKGROUND TO THE CHRISTIAN SPIRITUAL AND MYSTICAL TRADITION

The Gospels emphasise that you must enter into death in order to be reborn or resurrected. In various ways the journey of Jesus is a story of movement from death to life, of leaving darkness and emptiness to find meaning and purpose in life. Aspects of his journey may parallel our own, such as feelings of fear, alienation and abandonment, a loss of a sense of order or a sense of self.

For early Christians, a 'new birth' in the Spirit (John 3:3) through baptism was integral to being a spiritual person. The old person died and a new person was born; a new identity was formed through a new set of relationships involving church and the communion of the Spirit. The new identity given through the Eucharist (the Christian 'breaking of the bread', also known as Holy Communion) is about acquiring eternal life. It gives a new identity based on new relationships, like the Father–Son relationship of the Holy Trinity, and reaches the core of a person's being. Through grace (a freely given gift from God, not something freely chosen by the individual), the Christian is able to become what Christ is by nature.

This has tremendous implications for those in Twelve Step programs. The idea of a new identity and new relationships acquired through grace is intrinsic to the Twelve Step process. The old 'addict' self goes through a metamorphosis of sorts through Step One and this will eventually be replaced by the new yet more authentic self. A relationship with a Higher Power is formed, followed by relationships with others.

As in baptism, this new identity or new life, entered into by those who take Step One is a grace, a gift — something outside yourself has come into you. As Paul says, 'By grace you have been saved, through faith; and this is not of your own doing' (Ephesians 2:8). Paul had experienced this in his own life when, after persecuting Christians with the Romans for many years, he allegedly experienced a sudden and dramatic conversion. He believed he had been saved by grace. That is how he became a believer.

Paul's teachings contain many foundational concepts of Christian spirituality. The 'new person' appears through dying to self, 'a complete stripping of your natural self. This is circumcision according to Christ. You have been

buried with him by your baptism ...' (Colossians 2:6-19)
Paul also stressed:

> *You were to put aside your old self which belongs to*
> *your old way of life and is corrupted by following*
> *illusory desires. Your mind was to be renewed in*
> *spirit, so that you could put on the New [Person]*
> *that has been created on God's principles, in the*
> *uprightness and holiness of the truth.*
> *(Ephesians 4:22-25)*

A seminal thinker and mystic considered to be one of the first philosophers of the age, Origen (185–254 AD) was a teacher with the famous Alexandrian school of Greek philosophy. A pioneering humanist, Origen radically believed in the dignity of the human being and that everyone would reach salvation. Proficient in biblical studies as well as Greek culture, he was also very familiar with the Pagan and Jewish worlds, making him a link between faith and culture.

He lived during the turbulent times of the Roman Empire. The barbarian invasions were taking place and Christians were a persecuted sect and many were martyred for the cause. Persecuted and imprisoned before he died, like others after him, Origen affirmed the church view that the highest form of spirituality is martyrdom and any authentic form of spirituality involves some form of death, thus asceticism and martyrdom were the keys to spiritual enlightenment.

Instead of condemning this idea as an extreme act of self-denial and a stand against individualism, you can connect it to Step One by seeing it in a positive light by viewing Step One as a 'death' in the sense of dying to an old way of being, dying to the old self and to wilful attempts to control, this early Christian idea can be used to enhance your spirituality. You can find spiritual life through tragedy. A transformational process has begun where you die to the old, allowing the bringing in of the new.

TELLING THE STORY

Those in Twelve Step programs such as AA and people in recovery from addictions who tell others of their experiences remain connected to their story. This helps them to become contentedly free from their addiction as well as enabling them to work towards living a peaceful life.

Bible stories such as the Book of Exodus in the Old Testament tell us how a people became disconnected from God when they forgot their story and when self took over. The whole idea of remembering who we are is crucial. When you forget who you are or lose sight of your primary faith relationship, you lose focus and fail to stay connected with others. You fail to find meaning in life through a sustaining relationship with God. The 'exodus' experience is Israel's story of moving from bondage to freedom. Our own story is also one of God hearing our call and responding out of love: 'They cried out, and their appeal for rescue from their slavery rose up to God. He heard their groaning and remembered his covenant ...' (Exodus 2:23-25)

Bondage may be psychological, spiritual, emotional or a combination of all three. You could say that we are all born in 'Egypt', in bondage. We are called to be free, but realisation of freedom eludes us.[7] To be left with no hope is spiritual bondage. The prophet Isaiah emphasises this: 'I was bereft, exiled, turned out of my home ...' (Isaiah 49:21)

The exodus from the bondage of Egyptian oppression was also where Israel first received the 'creative call' of the Lord.[8] In admitting powerlessness you become receptive to a voice that calls you to be something beyond what you are. This in itself requires the creativity and grace of God and an openness to receive that grace.

INTO THE WILDERNESS: LETTING GO OF CONTROL

The biblical theme of exodus in the wilderness can also be paralleled with the desert experience in the Christian tradition. The Desert Fathers and Mothers, who were the early exponents of monasticism in the first centuries of Christianity before it became institutionalised, understood the wisdom of being in the desert to experience God acutely. This is a metaphor for what you can experience when entering the wilderness of the unknown. The admission of powerlessness can be an entry into the desert because it involves letting go of attempts to control. The idea of being in total control as the key to a successful life is one of the greatest delusions of modern society. It is also one of the most powerful delusions of someone in the grip of addiction.

You cannot control your addictions or vulnerabilities by yourself. You need help from a Higher Power and from others.

THE SOUL RETURNING TO GOD

Origen understood that conversion was about the soul returning to God. The conversion process begins with the Spirit stirring up the soul and making it aware of its need for conversion. Origen saw the progress of the soul as a pilgrimage, and through contemplation the soul eventually came to experience light, revelation and knowledge of the divine.

If you see the spiritual journeying of the Twelve Steps as a pilgrimage, Step One is the beginning of that journey out of the wilderness towards a spiritual home. One cannot avoid this time of living in the wilderness and being subject to feelings of complete helplessness. Matt

Talbot's story is an excellent example of this, as is one of Origen's homilies: 'You must come out of Egypt ... Pursue your spiritual journey through the wilderness until you come to the well which the kings dug ...'[9]

This is similar to what happens when you begin a journey with the Twelve Steps. God has a masterplan in your life, which will be revealed as time goes along:

> Moreover when the soul sets out from the Egypt of
> this life to go to the promised land, it necessarily
> goes by certain roads and ... observes certain stages
> that were made ready with the Father from the
> beginning ... my soul has long been on pilgrimage ...
> when the soul has returned to its rest, that is, to the
> father land in paradise, it will be taught more truly
> and will understand more truly what the meaning of
> its pilgrimage was.[10]

This is the nature of our journey.

THE QUEST FOR AUTHENTICITY INSTEAD OF PERFECTION

The sixteenth-century Spanish Carmelite mystic, St John of the Cross, wrote in his famous work *The Dark Night* that the soul should pass through two nights in order to attain union with God (in so far as it is possible in this life) through love. The first night, or purgation, involves the senses, the second, the spiritual part of the soul.[11] In another of his works, *The Ascent of Mount Carmel*, John talks of these as the 'active' night and 'passive' night respectively.[12] In contemporary terms the active night involves doing certain things to let go of what is unhelpful to you on your spiritual journey. The passive night is really God working in you, with you doing nothing, and may involve times of sheer emptiness.

John experienced his own 'rock bottom', his own 'long dark night of the soul', in 1577 when he was unjustly imprisoned for nine months and subjected to physical and mental abuse by some members of his own religious order, who were possibly threatened by his spiritual influence.[13] Despite this dreadful betrayal, his acute experience of love, pain and despair enhanced his understanding of how emptiness, often preceded by a purgation of sorts, can open us up to God. Through times of great suffering, John developed an enormous capacity to love and gained a more authentic spirituality.

He understood that this journey which takes you beyond self into the 'night' is a journey which ultimately brings you great gifts. When darkness and pain are present, the love of God is also present, bringing the soul companionship. This 'night' can be a journey to truth. Despite the times it may appear as chaos or a sense of abandonment, it can become a space for God to fill.

A WOUNDING ON THE ROAD TO UNITY

It is important to note that the idea of 'the ascent of the soul' is an image for spiritual progress. It is not about self-realisation via perfection or 'being good'. It is about union with God. John of the Cross knew that this is the one goal in the spiritual life. He was able to give solace to people such as the grieving mother and widow for whom he wrote *The Living Flame*, his hymn to the Holy Spirit. He understood the paradox that 'wounding' in some way would make one whole, for he had experienced this first hand in his own life. 'Wounding', in this sense, can mean psychological or emotional scarring such as the legacy of abuse, depression, loneliness or character weaknesses.

To admit that your life is unmanageable and that you are completely powerless is a huge step, involving leaving the road you know. In *The Ascent of Mount Carmel*, John writes:

> *As regards this road to union, entering on the road*
> *means leaving one's own road, or better,*
> *moving on to the goal;*
> *and turning from one's own mode implies entry into*
> *what has no mode, that is, God.*[14]

The acceptance of being beaten involves letting go of self. To let go of self you need to let go of what you know. This is part of our journey towards our more authentic self.

This is so that the really spiritual person
might understand ...
that the more annihilated she be for God ...
the more is she united with God,
and the greater the work she does.[15]

A JOURNEY OF UNCERTAINTY
AND FREEDOM

The journey you began with Step One is a journey in uncertainty. It has the potential to become your journey to freedom. The transformation of the individual reaches society on many levels, and that individual has the potential to affect the spiritual community by working on his or her own spiritual renewal. To enter fully into this transformation you may need to let go of your obsessions with the rational and with having control.

As Matt Talbot and Bill W experienced, events in our lives can mark the beginnings of self-discovery and self-transcendence. To experience Step One is to experience a necessary 'death' that starts you on a journey of transformation.

CHAPTER TWO

The Gradual Awakening

Step Two: Came to Believe that a Power Greater than
ourselves could restore us to sanity.

*Though I certainly didn't really expect anything, I
did make this frantic appeal: "If there be a God,
will he show Himself!" The result was instant,
electric, beyond description ...*
(Bill W)[1]

'Coming to believe' does not necessarily involve intellectual understanding or any understanding at all. It can sometimes be a combination of grace, simple heartfelt need and a desire to change. It comes out of the admission of powerlessness.

As Bill reflected:

We have to find a life in the world of grace and spirit, and this is certainly a new dimension for most of us. Surprisingly, our quest for this realm of being is not too difficult. Our conscious entry into it usually begins as soon as we have deeply confessed our personal powerlessness to go on alone, and have made our appeal to whatever God we think there is — or may be.[2]

GRADUAL TRANSFORMATION: THE WORLD OF GRACE AND SPIRIT

Your pilgrimage starts with the desire to connect. This new awakening happens when you have confessed your personal powerlessness. This can come about through a turning point such as mental breakdown, life crisis, admission of an addiction or simply a difficult personal problem, such as ending a relationship. For example, you may have a sudden moment when you are going about your daily life where you suddenly see yourself as you really are; you are able to see that a particular issue is a problem in your life. While the experience may not necessarily be dramatic it is profound in the effect it has. The process is the same as it involves throwing in the towel. A new dimension, a new experience of truth, comes about through total abandonment and letting go of everything you know. A new light has touched your life that was not there before. You begin to feel connected with yourself and to something outside yourself, a spiritual presence that acts mysteriously. You have entered the world of grace and spirit.

As there was for Bill W, there may be an epiphany, a holy moment, where a truth is revealed. Step Two is the awakening to that light when you glimpse something of what you could be, when you taste what freedom from self and from darkness might be like. The paradox is that in order to experience this freedom you must first enter darkness. Like someone about to dive into the cavernous depths of the unknown, this is the hard, terrifying part.

Taking Step Two may involve calling out to God for help in a crisis trusting that, despite your feelings of fear, all will be well even if you do not believe in God's existence or His/Her presence. Your call at this point of desperation may well be something like, 'If there is a God, help me', as it was for Bill and many others, or it may be a heart-wrenching plea such as Jesus gave in Gethsemane: 'Take this from me'. As it says in the *Big Book* of Alcoholics Anonymous, what has become clear for us at this point is that no human power can relieve our suffering, but God could and would if sought out.[3]

For some of us this step may involve letting go of images of God that are unhealthy or destructive, like a God of fear. However you perceive God or a Higher Power, you need a belief in the unconditional love and acceptance that God has for you. This does not involve your natural understanding or knowledge of God. It solely involves trust and is all about venturing into the unknown. This personal turning point transforms the present and can fill you with hope. Writer Morris West expresses this idea:

There comes a moment when you are aware that you are about to step out of light into darkness, out of the knowing into unknowing, without guarantee of return. It is a moment of clearness and stillness, in which you know, with strange certainty, that whatever is waiting to receive you is good, beneficent, loving. You are aware that you have been prepared for this moment, not by any action of your own, but by the gift of life itself, by the nature of life itself ... When, like Lazarus, I was recalled

from the darkness, when I stood blinded by the light
of a new day, I knew that my life could never be the
same again.[4]

The eventual revelation of your true self also comes about when you let go of your ego that deludes you into thinking you can be like God and are completely autonomous. 'Ego' in this sense is not to be confused with having healthy self-esteem or 'liking yourself' in contemporary terms. This 'letting go' is in contrast to the idea that the individual has the power to control everything in his or her life. It is the ultimate realisation that trying to control everything around you can fail. This does not mean you remain impotent or inactive in the world, it means acceptance of what you cannot change, such as certain situations, powerful emotional states that take over, and other people's behaviour.

As many will testify, the price for spiritual development is high. In overcoming the ego you often find yourself confronted by fear. You may find yourself overwhelmed by feelings of confusion, hopelessness, extreme emotional pain, or fear of madness. The reality is inescapable. You have to let go of everything you want to cling to so you can experience a spiritual rebirth.

Carl Jung alluded to the spiritual longing in human beings as far stronger than the drive of sexuality or the drive for power. It is our ultimate primal longing. In a letter to Bill W in the early days of AA, Jung wrote:

*I am strongly convinced that the evil principle
prevailing in this world, leads the unrecognised
spiritual need into perdition, if it is not counteracted
either by real religious insight, or by the protective
wall of human community.*[5]

Without God we are all vulnerable. This longing for spirituality is fraught with doubt. We suffer, says Jung, because we are victims of a profound uncertainty.[6]

Part of coming to believe or being restored to sanity or wholeness on a spiritual journey is the desire to fill that emptiness, to experience the fullness of reality. The belief that a power greater than yourself may restore you to sanity is the beginning. This hunger for something is particularly characteristic of taking Step Two. It involves a desire to connect that inspires you to search out communal support networks, supportive friends, spiritual guides or counselors. This really applies when you are going through major changes, such as walking away from a destructive situation. This step can bring with it the sense that our souls have something in store for us, 'We see only reflections in a mirror, we know only in part, but soon we shall know just as fully as we are known' (1 Corinthians 13:12).

The Christian concept of incarnation is about God entering fully into our humanity. This means experiencing the full gamut of the human condition, including human emotions at their darkest and brightest. In daily life this can mean realising that during all life's turning points you are not alone. There is some spirit outside and acting within that helps guide you along the way. Suffering is often part of that process and it is our natural instinct to resist or avoid it. You can look at this process and see that where there is chaos and helplessness, there is also order.

This does not in any way suggest that states such as suffering are needed or caused by God, but there is an overarching purpose for us in the world that surpasses them. In the beginning of Genesis in the Old Testament the cosmos is in chaos but God has a plan. Ultimately you will see how sometimes that chaos was necessary in order for God to enact His/Her plan.

If you cling to the old way of being and behaviours of the past that have not served you and tell yourself 'this is the way it is', then you are stifling the movement of creation in you. What you are challenged to do with this step is to allow things to grow, to move and enter into the new creation. The old order is gone and a new being is there to see (2 Corinthians 5:17). In accepting the challenge you become part of an eternal process of transformation that has been part of the mystical tradition since pre-Christian times. In Greco-Roman mythology the idea of transformation occurred in such stories as snakes turning into stones.[7] In Hellenistic mystery religions the idea of transformation involved the freeing of the body from the bonds of the material world to bring about a change in spiritual nature, in effect, the divinisation of the human being.[8]

In the New Testament, Paul's idea of transformation is similar to this. The human being is transformed into the seen image of God. You do not immediately recognise this new reality of being, but it guides your future behaviour. This transformation is an invisible process manifesting itself in the life of the individual. Unlike the Hellenistic concept, the individual cannot bring this about by himself or herself. Only Christ, God or a Higher Power can reshape human beings:

> *All of us, with our unveiled faces like mirrors*
> *reflecting the glory of the Lord, are being*
> *transformed into the image that we reflect in*
> *brighter and brighter glory; this is the working of*
> *the Lord who is the Spirit.*
> *(2 Corinthians 3:18)*

This is a key issue for people in Twelve Step programs. Translated for everyday life, it means you cannot totally change yourself as it is only through opening yourself to the presence of the Spirit that you can undergo this dramatic change. This requires the grace of God.

CHAPTER THREE

LETTING GO — A STEP TOWARDS LIFE

Step Three: Made a decision to hand our will and our lives over to the care of God as we understood him.

Take, O Lord and receive
My entire liberty,
My memory, my understanding and my whole will.
All that I am and all that I possess
You have given me:
I surrender it all to You
To be disposed of according to Your will.
Give me only Your love and Your grace;
With these I will be rich enough,
And will desire nothing more.
(St Ignatius)[1]

MELISSA'S STORY

If I look back on my journey I see how the intellectual and rational dominated my thinking and suppressed my deep-seated depression. It took an experience where I became aware of Spirit, something completely outside myself, to allow me to change, which helped me live from the heart.

I battled depression on and off for years. I still had the desire to stay sober, but this was coupled with a deep-seated malaise. Years of not listening to what was in my heart had taken its toll. A pervading darkness took root within me.

A combination of things had happened — I had just lost someone I loved, I had isolated myself from many friendships and I hated my job. There had been a continual eroding of my self-esteem over many years. I became plagued with thoughts of suicide and I felt totally helpless in the face of these thoughts. I thought, what can I do? The underlying question through it all for me was: if my life has no meaning, why am I here? I felt powerful dark forces pushing me to the edge. My thoughts of suicide were no longer thoughts, they became plans.

I felt like my mind was separating from my body. I had heard many people who had attempted suicide speak of this phenomenon. In that inevitable downward spiral I could see myself spinning totally out of control. I felt completely unresponsible for my actions. Part of me felt completely insane. I knew it was only a matter of time before things would go one way or the other.

I saw psychiatrists and counsellors. When I eventually told a counselor about the truth of my life — all the pent-up anger and feelings of loss, shame and betrayal — I felt a peaceful reassuring presence envelop me. She suggested I take some time out, perhaps at a retreat centre, and get some rest and process what had happened.

I took the plunge and did a silent retreat for five days. I was told to meditate on the resurrection, something which I had never had much interest in, and always had a great deal of difficulty understanding on an intellectual level. What did 'raised from the dead' mean anyway?

What happened was an awakening of heart, a spiritual experience of total conversion. It was not unlike that of Bill W. It felt like the wind, like a Spirit coming into my soul and body. It changed me totally; I walked away from that experience a completely different person. I still had the same problems, but had no expectations about my future and was filled with enormous joy. It was almost as if nothing could ever hurt me again which, of course, was not the case, but that's what it felt like. So in effect the counselor was right; I had to be born again, and that meant nothing less than being born in the Spirit.

That transforming moment left God at the centre of everything. It was a feeling of being connected. For hours after that I felt a total surrender, it was as if I saw only God.

Not surprisingly life has never been the same since.

~———~

Many spiritual writers have reflected on how suffering can bring you closer to God and open you up to the workings of the Spirit. As Melissa's story shows, all the effort of self-will and determination to beat whatever demons you are battling, be they addictions or psychic meltdown, results in nothing. The only way through the problem and out of the desolation is to hand over control of your life to a higher force and to realise that this force, which ultimately is God, is the only thing that can turn around your life. You realise that your only hope is this loving God who you may not understand, but is there for you.

After taking Step Two, Step Three opens the door by bringing about a gradual openness and willingness to allow the true self to emerge with the help of God. Essentially this new journey is the beginning of your search for unity and wholeness. It is also the beginning of freedom. 'The more we become willing to depend upon a Higher Power, the more independent we actually are.'[2]

You are more connected to human beings by being more open to others and more able to let go of the fear of what might happen if you fall apart. Your prayer is:

God, I offer myself to Thee, to build with me and to do with me as Thou wilt. Relieve me of the bondage of self, that I may better do Thy will. Take away my difficulties, that victory over them may bear witness to those I would help of Thy power, Thy love, and Thy way of life. May I do your will always.[3]

Those who have experienced the trauma of abandonment, helplessness or despair know only too well that to hand one's life over to God completely is a decision that carries with it the sense of entering into the unknown along with a feeling of relief. While falling into the unknown can be a fearful proposition, to go back to where you have come from is unbearable, however familiar it may be. Your destiny is to press forwards into the unknown, without expectations, knowing you are making a conscious choice for God. With this step you may be given a glimpse that the quality of your life depends on the quality of your relationship with God. Even if it is only a mustard seed of faith, it is this which helps feed your soul.

This conscious choice for God under the circumstances of an unknown future is the crux of the spiritual life. It forces you to let go of expectations and can awaken your

heart to love and allows you to be reborn in the Spirit. As
Jesus tells Nicodemus:

> *In all truth I tell You,*
> *no one can see the kingdom of God*
> *without being born from above ...*
> *The wind blows where it pleases;*
> *you can hear its sound,*
> *but you cannot tell where it comes from*
> *or where it is going.*
> *So it is with everyone who is born of the Spirit.*
> *(John 3:3–8)*

The idea of the pilgrimage of the soul is one that affected
early monasticism and later medieval spirituality. As with
Melissa's story, it involves the idea of moving away from
your 'home', a place of comfort in the spiritual sense, to a
place you do not know, 'a region of unlikeness'.

The idea of the pilgrimage of the soul has prayer as its
essence. Your prayer life, which you begin with Step
Three, is really a pilgrimage to your own centre, a journey
to your heart, but you do not yet fully know this place.
Taking Step Three is a pivotal part of your pilgrimage,
your Twelve Step journey.

An essential part of the Christian concept of moving
away from an old way of life to a new way of life through
the action of God is the whole idea of withdrawing into

self for contemplation. This was an idea that was establishing itself during the time of Christ, particularly among some monastic Jewish sects. In the Christian tradition, particularly from the time of St Augustine (late fourth century) up until at least the twelfth century, the concept of a threefold withdrawal underpinning the spiritual life involved the idea of withdrawing from the world, withdrawing within the self, in order to experience God above the self. That is, going into the self to go above the self to go beyond the self. This idea was also embraced by people such as Origen, and the desert monks in Egypt and surrounding areas before the time of Augustine. It has been absorbed in the contemplative tradition for centuries. This concept is still with us.

DESERT SPIRITUALITY

The idea that the desert is a secluded wilderness where we face both our unknown selves and our unknown future has always been part of Christian spirituality. As with Melissa's experience, it is no mere metaphor that space and emptiness can open us up to God. It was in the desert that Jesus faced temptation by the devil. With its vastness and emptiness the desert calls to mind the solitary nature of the individual's spiritual journey. In the desert you confront your own emptiness and fear and find yourself face to face with the awesome mystery, which cannot be named or understood. You are forced to rely on God, the God of your own understanding.

The roots of monasticism lie in the Egyptian desert of the fourth century. The Desert Fathers and Mothers' way of life was 'being' through contemplation and action. It was a way of life that was 'caught' rather than 'taught'.

These people laid down essential tenets of Christian spirituality that still remain, ideas such as renouncing the world, letting go of ego, letting go of self, suffering as part of life and preparing for journeying with God. The desert took on the most real and stark dimensions and the Desert Fathers and Mothers possessed an all too vivid awareness of the evil that exists in the world and the need for a preparedness to combat it. The two primary virtues that shone as goals for the early Church Fathers and Mothers were humility and charity.

ST ANTONY

A discussion of monasticism could not go by without referring to the man considered to be the source of it: St Antony of Egypt. He was often called 'the father of Christian monasticism' and his story truly embodies the emptying that is involved in going into the desert. In 269 AD, at the age of twenty, he responded to the reading of Matthew 19:21, 'If you would be perfect, go and sell all that you have and give to the poor; and come, follow me', by going out into the

Egyptian desert and living as a hermit.

In seeking perfection, Antony renounced his inheritance, lived on the desert margins of the village and sought guidance from other holy men, becoming renowned as a healer. Antony epitomised the concept of 'letting go absolutely'. Some of his calls were extreme:

> Hate the world and all that is in it.
> Hate all peace that comes from the flesh.
> Renounce this life, that you may be alive to God ...
> Suffer hunger, thirst, nakedness ...
> test yourselves ...[4]

Antony's values, such as renouncing attachments, can be applied to today's world — not to place material or other attachments and the cares of this world before your relationship with God. For today's world his message can be interpreted as 'be in the world but not of it'.

The idea that the monks were engaged in a 'spiritual battle' in the desert was not so naïve. Through fighting the battles within themselves, fighting against their own passions and recognising their own struggles and brokenness they were able to become closer to the reality of themselves. In today's world, we do not necessarily engage in such a fight. For example, we do not demonise normal parts of our humanity, like sexuality, as the monks did. In contemporary terms the monks' message can be seen as 'do not be a mental and emotional slave to your possessions and desires', but rather strive for emotional detachment from them and put your desire for truth and closeness to God as your primary focus.

For the monastics there was a continual process of 'compunction', or a piercing in their hearts, which made them aware of their sinfulness and need for mercy. This was often followed by repentance. The desert was a place of freedom as well as a place of conflict within the self. The 'demons', real or imagined, visual or internal, acted as spurs causing the monk to be 'stripped of all things' and led closer to God. Dealing with this conflict enhanced and strengthened their spiritual awareness, moving them along their path of intimacy with God. This thinking, while on one level dramatic and extreme, wisely moved away from the rationalisation of the Greeks, which focused on independent intellectual interpretation of the empirical world. A writer of the times observed of these people: 'It is clear to all who dwell there, that through them the world is kept in being'.[5]

In today's world a crisis, personal breakdown or experience such as Melissa's might cause you to face your own 'desert' experience and lead you to be 'stripped of all things'. Such a turning point might cause you to be more honest with someone or with yourself about what is really going on in your life and, in the process, bring about greater spiritual awareness.

In this rationalistic world you might also apply Christ's dictum: 'Seek first the Kingdom of God and all things will come to pass' (Matthew 6:33) or in Twelve Step terms: 'See to it that your relationship with him is right, and great events will come to pass for you and countless others'.[6] Jesus' words also give us guidance: 'When the Spirit of truth comes he will guide you into all the truth' (John 16:13).

This means that when a spiritual relationship is your primary focus the other problems of life are easier to manage. This does not make you immune to suffering, but places greater meaning on the bigger picture in your life and bestows a greater capacity to deal with problems when prayer and action are combined.

ST BENEDICT

Another famous monastic worthy of attention is St Benedict, considered the father of Western monasticism. He was a young man when he was sent to Rome to study. Benedict was repelled by the goings on in the city and sought solitude by fleeing to a cave in Subiaco where he lived a hermit's life for three years. Encountering much hostility and jealousy from religious leaders due to the number of disciples who followed him, he was forced to move away from his sanctuary several times. He founded his famous monastery on the summit of Monte Cassino in 525.

His Rule has had a dramatic influence on Christian spirituality. Unlike the extreme asceticism of the Desert Fathers and Mothers, the monasticism practised by St Benedict suggested balance while still maintaining the essential monastic virtues of daily prayer, singleness of heart and humility. The beginning of the prologue of the Benedictine Rule parallels Step Three in its emphasis on letting go of self. 'If you are ready to give up your own will, once and for all ... And in the Prayer too we ask God that his "will be done" in us' (Matthew 6:10).

Benedict espoused the constant ideal of conversion and contemplation: a gradual turning towards God that is not only your continual goal, but your continual sustenance. The Rule echoes how you grow and find true self-fulfilment, heightening the awareness of the Christ within. 'Let us open our eyes to the light that comes from God, and our ears to the voice from heaven that every day calls out this charge: If you hear his voice today, do not harden your hearts ...'[7]

By moving beyond the comprehensible you go to the unknown where God lives. Mystics such as the anonymous author of *The Cloud of Unknowing* understood this. In order to know God mystically through love you must abandon what your imagination and pre-conceived ideas tell you. Likewise John of the Cross, Pseudo-Dionysius and others understood that prayer and emptiness through the *via negativa*, the path of nothingness, were ways to God.

When starting your pilgrimage of the heart with Step Three you are moving from the known to the unknown. You are attempting to empty yourself of all past ideas that have not served you. An example of this might be the need to let go of an attitude of cynicism or a 'me against them' attitude in the world. Alternatively it might be the need to let go of constant distrust of those closest to you so that you can live more freely. The *Big Book* offers an important maxim on this: 'Some of us have tried to hold onto our old ideas, but the result was nil until we let go absolutely'.[8]

The only way to deal with either suffering or joy is to enter into it with faith, to walk with it knowing that God is with you. This is what can bring the connectedness you long for, as the lack of this connectedness can bring so many ills, such as depression and mental illness.

To walk in the mystery of the spiritual life means to walk in uncertainty. This is the path of true faith. The prophet Isaiah reminds us of the bigger picture of mystery in our lives: 'No need to remember past events, no need to think about what was done before. Look I am doing something new, now it emerges. Can you not see it?' (Isaiah 43:18–19)

CHAPTER FOUR

LOOKING AT THE PAST

Step Four: Made a searching and fearless moral inventory of ourselves.

Jesus said, 'If you bring forth what is within you, what you have will save you. If you do not have that within you, what you do not have within you [will destroy] you.'
(The Gospel Of Thomas)[1]

BRIAN'S STORY

If I cannot begin to know myself I cannot begin to heal myself, so the basic step of this self-knowledge begins with a material confession. Before I confess to anyone else I must confess to myself, acknowledge who I really am and what my fears are. If I am to put my wellbeing above everything else I must start with a concrete list of 'symptoms' to deal with.

I came from a poor home on the unfashionable side of town. I had a violent alcoholic father. I used humour to cope with pain for most of my life. This humour was part of me wanting to hide who I really was and what I was really feeling.

For me, Step Four was ridding myself of the yoke across my shoulders. It was as though a huge burden had been lifted from me. I got back the spring in my step. After I had listed all my concrete resentments, I realised the burden I was carrying was my toxic shame and secrets.

What does a fearless and thorough moral inventory involve? In essence it involves honesty, which is an essential part of humility. Fundamentally this step is about getting to know your own weaknesses and strengths. It is also the beginning of awareness of how the admission of these things can strengthen and free you.

This admission involves asking God to remove whatever self-will has blocked you off from Him/Her.[2] In contemporary psychological terms, this may include 'toxic shame' or 'secrets', or events that fill you with guilt or shame: those things that dominate your life now, regardless of whether or not you were responsible for them. Step Four is also about letting go of 'inordinate' or 'disordered attachments': those obsessive attachments to people, places and things that keep you in chains.

All this takes humility and a willingness to see yourself as you truly are. This leads to a further letting go of self and starts you on the way to becoming less self-centered, which is an essential part of any authentic spiritual process. Once you deal with those things that separate you from God, you get closer to your more authentic self.

The Christian idea of 'compunction', where monks and others who were committed to a spiritual path felt a piercing in their hearts that made them aware of their faults and their potential to be free of them, is not only the domain of monastics. For many people such feelings happen after taking Step Three. There is spiritual peace and commitment but there is also an awareness of those conflicts within the self that still remain. It is during Step Four that these issues are addressed.

This process of moral inventory may lead to either a formal or informal confession or a Step Five where you tell someone else the story of your life — how it has been for you, who has hurt you, and how you have reacted. On the other hand, it can be as simple as asking God to help you become aware of the distortions of your life and to help you to let go of them.

You specifically look at things like fears, resentments and misdirected instincts, which include those drives within you, like the drive for personal recognition or power, that cause you to fluctuate between a constant desire to satiate your ego and a state of low self-esteem. You also look at where you have tried to rely on personal empowerment:

> We reviewed our fears thoroughly.
> We put them on paper, even though we had no
> resentment in connection with them.
> We asked ourselves why we had them.
> Wasn't it because self-reliance
> failed us?[3]

Those on the verge of completing this step may experience intense feelings of desolation, despair or anxiety. To admit your own past failures or weaknesses or your reaction to those of others and their effect on you can be a daunting process. The resulting desolation can play a crucial role in your spiritual growth by emptying you and making you more vulnerable and open to the work of God.

It is important to remember that the spiritual life is not necessarily about denial of any kind or about forfeiting your humanity in any way. All aspects of yourself need to be embraced in the spiritual life. After all, the incarnation is about the Word made flesh, God in the form of your humanity. Remember that Jesus Christ emptied himself like a slave (Philippians 2:6–11).

The contemplative tradition does stress renunciation, detachment and self-mortification as part of the progress towards illumination and the union with God. Renunciation and detachment are helpful ideas for a contemporary spiritual journey, particularly for those in Twelve Step programs. You do need to release yourself from things such as destructive self-will if you are to progress in the spiritual life. By letting go of those attachments that hold back your spirit you give your heart more freedom.

ST IGNATIUS AND THE EXAMINATION OF CONSCIENCE

The moral inventory of Step Four is similar to the 'examination of conscience' idea espoused by St Ignatius Loyola, a soldier wounded in a siege in the Spanish town of Pamplona in 1521 and taken to the castle of Loyola to recover. It was during his long convalescence that he experienced a spiritual conversion after reading *A Life of Christ and the Saints*. His period of penance, meditation and revelation led him to put together his Spiritual Exercises. He founded the Jesuit order aimed at serving people and leading them to God, in particular, self-conversion leading to the service of others.

These exercises extend over four weeks. The first week involves attending to the Mystery of Salvation. (This may be understood as acknowledgment of your own failures and frailties and the gift of God's mercy.) The second week involves attending to the life of Christ up to his entry into Jerusalem on Palm Sunday (a deeper process of moral inventory). The third attends to his Passion (the suffering and death of Christ) and involves meditating on those things that emerge from your inventory and how they have affected your life. The fourth week is devoted to his Resurrection and Ascension where, out of the love you have received, you resolve to give yourself totally.[4]

Ignatius defines 'spiritual exercises' as any method of

examining your conscience – meditation, contemplation or mental or vocal prayer – or any method of handling your spiritual life. Spiritual exercises call to the soul to remove unhealthy obsessions, to seek and find the will of God in the management of your life and to find your role in the Paschal mystery (the life, death and resurrection of Christ).[5] It is easy to see Steps Four and Five as being similar to this process of examination.

You ask God's grace to come and help you do this step, reminding yourself that God's grace is the action of God lovingly calling a response from you. Often, writing things down is the best way to do this. Ignatius talks about a five-point plan that is part of an 'Examination of Conscience'. Firstly, you thank God for the good things in your life. Secondly, you ask God's help to know what your personal failures or weaknesses are. Thirdly, you pray that you are able to acknowledge your own character weaknesses regularly in word and deed. Fourthly, you ask God's mercy for these faults in thought, word and deed. And finally, with God's grace, you begin to plan some program of reparation for these things, closing with a prayer such as the 'Our Father'.[6] (The last two points parallel what you desire to achieve in Step Five.)

Ignatius mentions that confession, a tangible expression of God's forgiveness as happens in the Catholic tradition, may be a good way of completing this examination of conscience (very similar to Step Five), although it is not essential. Spiritual confrontation can cure someone's apathy and hearten them in their progress in the spiritual life.[7] Letting go of all obsessive attachments may be difficult and will never be done completely. Many of us have baggage from our life experiences, such as our childhoods. Loneliness, repressed anger or shame are some examples of these attachments. Those attachments that have caused great conflict and separated you from God in the past and have the potential to separate you from God in the present are worthy of attention.

Two key concepts, desolation and consolation, are common to Ignatian spirituality. Spiritual desolation is a state where you feel lacking in faith, hope or love. It may involve feeling depressed or being in a state of darkness, turmoil or restlessness. It can also bring a brief feeling of deceptive satisfaction if you succumb to acts like promiscuity or gambling in an attempt to feed your emptiness. Ironically, spiritual desolation is often followed by feelings of increased emptiness. Consolation, on the other hand, is when you feel stirred in your soul towards love of God and of others for their own sake and for no other reason.[8] The three characteristics of both states are the feeling itself, such as feeling either distressed or peaceful; the source of that feeling, a situation or God; and the consequences of that feeling in your life, such as a movement towards God or away from God.

Before, during or after Step Four, you may feel any one

of these states. In a desolate state there may be anxiety about the nature of the material to be shared and a feeling of worthlessness or emptiness. In a state of consolation there may be a feeling of peace and love of God. Alternately there may be an appropriate feeling of sadness when you look at where you have harmed yourself or others.

Ignatius advises against making major decisions when you are in a state of desolation. It is not hard to see why. Feelings of intense despair or hopelessness can easily distort your reason. It is best in this case to wait until you have discussed with a friend, confessor or the recipient of Step Five a course of action that should be taken on some matters. Often these times are a call to engage in deeper prayer for guidance.[9]

One way of dealing with the psychological resistance you might feel before completing Step Four is to do what Ignatius suggests for those starting on major life-changing decisions. Imagine being on your deathbed and confessing the truth of your life. What would you say?[10]

In engaging in a fearless and thorough inventory it is important to remember several things. John of the Cross reminds us that only God is able to comprehend those aspects of humanity which lie deep within. If you find yourself besieged by any feelings of uncomfortableness or desolation, you might remind yourself of his words, 'To come to the knowledge you have not, you must go by a way in which you know not ...'[11]

Successfully completing Step Four involves being open to the movement of your heart and to God's grace. This step is about handing over in faith. The cosmos may seem to be in chaos but God has a plan for you. If you are on the verge of doing Step Four you may feel chaotic, fearful or reluctant to go forward but this is where trust comes in.

If it were not for the life crises, difficulties, addictions and so on that come up, there would be no need for this step. As it says in the Old Testament, sometimes you find yourself afflicted in order that what is in your heart might be made known. This follows on from the desert experience.

Remember the long road by which ... your God led
you for forty years in the desert, to humble you, to
test you and know your inmost heart ...
He humbled you, he made you feel hunger, he fed you
with manna which neither you nor your ancestors
had ever known, to make you understand that human
beings live not on bread alone but on every word that
comes from the mouth of Yahweh [God].
(Deuteronomy 8:2–3)

JOHN CASSIAN AND THE GOAL OF SINGLENESS OF HEART

Following in the footsteps of his master Evagrius (a disciple of the Eastern desert tradition), one of the great figures of monasticism, John Cassian, saw the monk's way of life as an inner journey. This journey begins with the reverence for God and passes through compunction to renunciation of self. In this inner life your goal is singleness of heart, seeking only God. In carrying out this goal, simplicity and humility are your foundation stones.[12] It is with this idea of purity of heart that you can approach Step Four and later Step Five, or the formal rite of confession with a friend, spiritual guide, priest or advisor. For they alone will open you up to the grace of God and change you forever.

CHAPTER FIVE

THE OLD SELF STRIPPED AWAY

Step Five: Admitted to God, to ourselves, and to another human being, the exact nature of our wrongs.

Jesus said, 'Know what is in front of your face, and what is hidden from you will be disclosed to you. For there is nothing hidden that won't be revealed.'
(The Gospel Of Thomas)[1]

If you make my word your home
you will indeed be my disciples;
you will come to know the truth,
and the truth will set you free.
(John 8: 31, 32)

JULIA'S STORY

When I told the truth of my life to someone else I realised that much of my life's problems stemmed from repressed anger and the feeling of deep shame about the way I felt. Often what is unknown lies lurking as an enemy. When you know your enemy, you can give shape to your fears. When I did Step Five my confession enabled me to express how I felt about people, places and things and left me free to allow God to come into my life.

I realised that most of my problems were caused by a combination of the traits I was born with and the emotional damage of my circumstances. When I was able to give a voice to all the events of my past, I saw it all the more clearly and owned it. Underpinning most things were self-centredness, repressed anger, and fear, specifically fear of abandonment. I had always felt completely abandoned and emotionally neglected. Looking at the past opened the door, but most of all it gave me insight into why I felt the way I did. I felt forgiven.

Realising and naming your own woundedness is part of the journey to becoming whole. This is Step Five, a step that can also open you up to receive love into your life, particularly the love of a power outside yourself. As John of the Cross' poem *The Living Flame of Love* testifies:

Flame alive compelling,
yet tender past all telling,
reaching the secret centre of my soul!
Since now evasion's over,
Finish your work, my Lover,
Break the last thread,
wound me and make me whole![2]

As Julia's story shows, to admit defects (those personality characteristics that have caused you problems in life) or to admit how you really feel about what has happened in your life requires ego deflation.

Dissolving the ego is another term for letting go of self-will. To reiterate, self-will is not to be confused with looking after yourself or self-love, it is the delusion of self-mastery over the world and over your life. It is what blocks you off from the light of God by telling you that personal empowerment alone is the key to happiness. The Serenity Prayer gives reassurance at this time for you know you cannot change the past, you can only change the here and now.

God grant me the serenity,
to accept the things I cannot change,
courage to change the things I can,
and the wisdom to know the difference.[3]

You might see this step as the Spirit calling you to some greater good. In effect God is calling you in love towards your truth. If you have lived far apart from your truth this step can turn things around. Letting go of the ego which stops you looking at the truth is a start. The gradual movement of your heart, the conversion towards life, is what is happening in this step.

A 'shadow history' is the side of yourself that you may not have been aware of, such as ego disguised in the form of altruism, that you give out of self-interest. As you discover your shadow history with Step Five you become more integrated and more discerning in finding out where God is leading you.

Your inability to address your authentic self can lead to spiritual impoverishment. Some of the hidden sayings of Jesus found in the Gospel of Thomas (one of the gnostic gospels discovered in the twentieth century) give an important message in this regard.

Jesus said, '... the [Kingdom] is inside you and
outside you. When you know yourselves then you
will be known, and you will understand that you are

children of the living Father. But if you do
not know yourselves, then you live in
*poverty and you are the poverty.*⁴

Bill W reiterates this point:

I must look inside myself, to free myself. I must call
upon God's power to face the person I've feared the
most, the true me, the person God created me to be.
Unless I can or until I do, I will always be running,
and never be truly free. I ask God daily to
*show me such a freedom!*⁵

As you complete this process of revealing yourself to another person remember that you may see things about your life at certain times and not at others. Other issues may present themselves later, so aim for honesty not perfection. You cannot address all your life problems at once. You are looking at what needs to be addressed in your life now and what has come up for you.

John of the Cross emphasises this need to progress at your own spiritual pace. In your dialogue with God, God treats you 'with order, gentleness, and in a way that suits the soul', 'little by little', and 'carries each person along a different road'.⁶

To reconcile with one another means to make things right. In this process of reconciliation you are dealing with the nature of your wrongs and what is truly behind your actions. In taking this step you need to watch out for misdirected guilt, in other words, over-scrupulous guilt about things you may have done, and look at what is behind your misdirected instincts. As Julia's story reflects, the force you often discover behind your actions is fear, particularly fear of abandonment.

In taking on this process you may come up against feelings of fear or desolation as you reveal yourself. You begin this step by asking God to 'remove our fear and direct our attention to what He would have us be. At once, we commence to outgrow fear.'[7]

The need for self-knowledge can be powerful. By telling another your deepest defects, the things that really disturb you, such as distressing and humiliating memories or secrets, you allow yourself the opportunity to find relief from the anxiety, remorse and depression caused by these things.

Often this step is about emerging from isolation and feeling at one with God, with others and with yourself for the first time in your life. Not only does this step often open up the channels of forgiveness, it has the potential to give you a feeling of true kinship with God.

A sensitive spiritual advisor, sponsor or confidante may help with this process, but ultimately it is in the hands of God. You just know you have begun your liberation from the bondage of self.

How can you quantify such an amazing feeling? Here you face the deep divisions within your soul and embark further on a process of finding unity and wholeness. This requires truly letting go.

The long-term benefits cannot be counted, for 'when we are honest with another person, it confirms that we have been honest with ourselves and with God'.[8] If this step is done to the best of your ability, your inner dignity, 'a most beautiful and finely wrought image of God',[9] can be seen.

HUMILITY

Humility is an integral part of the spiritual life and it is important to define it. It is not to be confused with allowing yourself to be exploited. It is about honesty, about discussing yourself and holding nothing back.[10] Only after telling the truth of your life and acknowledging your weaknesses and vulnerabilities, rather than being driven by egoistic concerns about what others might think, can progress be made. 'It amounts to a clear recognition of what and who we really are, followed by a sincere attempt to become what we could be.'[11]

Just as a capacity for humility and self-emptying is a prerequisite for facing who you really are, it is also a step on the pathway to God. The false self gradually gives way to the true self that is hiding. Another of the Desert

Fathers, John of Lycopolis, talks about the selfish, false and illusory self which you can mistake for your real self. A priority is to pray to God 'so that standing before God who is darkness [unknowable] the false self may be stripped away and the true image and likeness of God within be revealed'.[12] To start to find this true self you need do what St Benedict suggests and 'Listen ... with the ear of your heart'.[13]

One of the Benedictine vows is for continual conversion of life, a conversion to a way of seeing, as the blind man pleads in the gospel stories, '[Lord] let me see again ...' (Mark 10:51 and Matthew 20:33).

This is part of your continual call for conversion, to let go of your old way of life and embrace the new through the action of God. Your *conversatio*, conversion and turning towards God, is an ongoing process where you also aim for *metanoia*, the Greek word meaning conversion of mind and heart.

Before completing this step you might have felt alienated from your own centre. Your self-centredness may have caused you to do many wrong things or at the very least caused you unhappiness. Conversion helps free you from this darkness and leads you to become more other-centred. This, in a sense, is what can be understood by the Catholic sacrament of 'penance'. You are moving from a place of being fixated on self to a place where you are fixated on the Other, God, Jesus Christ or a Higher

Power. Discovering your centre in God is true conversion and reconnects you to your own true centre. As the beatitudes say, 'blessed are the pure in heart: they shall see God'. (Matthew 5:8)

Benedictine John Main expresses this as:

> *Our centre is in God. To love God is to have our centre of consciousness in him. Just as his love for us is manifested in the Incarnation by which he, by emptying himself, placed his centre in us.*[14]

With this step you explore the responses of your heart. You look at where your heart is divided, where freedom and non-freedom operate. The word of God (in Christian terms this means the Spirit of Christ in our hearts, in scripture, and in the Holy Spirit acting in the world) judges the movements and secret intentions of the heart:

> *The word of God is something alive and active; it cuts more incisively than any two-edged sword: it can seek out the place where soul is divided from spirit, or joints from marrow; it can pass judgement on secret emotions and thoughts. No created thing is hidden from him; everything is uncovered and stretched fully open to the eyes of the one to whom we must give account of ourselves.*
> *(Hebrews 4:12–13)*

STEP FIVE WITH ST IGNATIUS

Steps Four and Five are steps of moral inventory and parallel the Ignatian exercises closely, so St Ignatius' approach may be helpful for those who want to go deeper with this process. In the first week of the Ignatian spiritual exercises you ask for God's grace as you consider the effects of your actions on your life, the personal implications of what has happened, and respond with the appropriate movements of heart. Ignatius then advises that you have a dialogue with the mystery of salvation, in this sense, contemplating God's grace in the midst of who you really are. Then you reflect on Christ crucified, and you speak your mind and heart to him. This dialogue may involve asking for consultation, a personal favour, or advice on how to handle a difficult situation.[15] It may be as simple as asking God's grace to guide you in the right direction or to give you the right words to say in resolving a conflict you have with someone.

In Twelve Step terms, this might mean asking for guidance on a specific situation. For example, if you neglected your spouse because you were busy pursuing your addiction, an apology might be in order. *The Big Book* advises that 'in meditation, we ask God what we should do about each specific matter. The right answer will come, if we want it.'[16]

You might look at where spiritual consolation and desolation are occurring in your life and where these attitudes come from. To what ends do they lead you?[17] If they do not lead you to God then perhaps you need to let go of some of them, or at least move on from them.

In Ignatian thinking, after you work to remove some of the addictions and distortions of your life, you are freer to talk with Jesus (or in Twelve Step terms, God or your Higher Power) and allow him to immerse his heart and mind in you. This is what often takes place in the second week of the Ignatian exercises (often considered the most important week). You are seeking to immerse yourself into the mystery of Christ. In contemplating the mystery of Christ, God or your Higher Power, Ignatius desires that you use not just your mind, will and imagination, but also that you contemplate the mystery of yourself in order to allow God to manage your life. This may be a powerful spiritual process developed from trusting and letting go. It may also be seen as measuring your own life against the life, sufferings, death and resurrection of Jesus, and the Paschal mystery.

In Ignatian understanding you are seeking your role in the Paschal mystery, the spiritual process of the life, death and resurrection of Christ who emptied himself to God. In Twelve Step terms you are also asking God's grace to guide you in your life from hereon in and to not let your shortcomings drive you.

As Ignatius says, you should ask God to let you know how you can serve him.[18] A contemporary reading of this notes, 'While I continue to contemplate his [Jesus'] life, let me begin to examine myself and ask to what state of life or to what kind of lifestyle is God ... leading me?'[19] For example, you might be a workaholic seeking more balance in your life.

In the second week of the exercises, you are also encouraged to meditate on 'two standards' or in contemporary terms 'two leaders, two strategies'. This is essentially an awareness of good versus evil, but not necessarily 'evil' as understood in modern-day terms, rather, a tendency to make yourself the centre of everything rather than seeing God as the centre. You ask for knowledge of how you may be deceived and for help in guarding yourself against this deceit.[20]

Ignatius is emphatic that you should know your own weaknesses. He also uses the analogy of a military general, an image he would have been familiar with as an ex-soldier. If you know your own weaknesses you know how you can be attacked.[21]

In the New Testament, you are reminded:

My dear friends, not every spirit is to be trusted,
but test the spirits to see whether they are from God
for many false prophets are at large in the world.
(1 John 4:1)

It is also wise to remember that any desolation you may feel doing this step may be a means of purifying and deepening your love for God. It plays a crucial role in spiritual growth. For example, John Cassian, the fourth/fifth century writer who was inspired by the monks of Egypt and later took that wisdom to the West, talks about how compunction, which produces movements of the heart in the hidden recesses of the spirit, can later emerge as an unspeakable joy.[22]

The consolation of tears (which Ignatius also speaks of) can also occur while completing Step Five:

> *Sometimes the soul lies low, hidden in the depths of silence ... with unspeakable groanings it pours out its longings to God. And sometimes it fills us with such sorrow and grief that it can only shake it off by melting into tears.*[23]

Self-knowledge is crucial on the Twelve Step journey. It is also a way to compensate against desolation. Not only do you need to know who you are in order to be free, you also desire to be known intimately by God. This knowledge only comes partially and slowly. For,

> *Now we see only reflections in a mirror, mere riddles,*
> *but then we shall be seeing face to face.*
> *Now I can know only imperfectly*
> *but then I shall know just as fully*
> *as I am myself known.*
> *(1 Corinthians 13:12)*

A resolute change of heart and a resolve to allow God to manage your life is the potential that is found in this step. The reparation of wrongs comes at a later stage, but at this point it may be simply appropriate to know you are forgiven by God and be more willing to forgive those who have wronged you and willing to forgive yourself. This latter gift is most important.

The story of the Prodigal Son (Luke 15:11–32) in the New Testament also has an important message. The wayward son was received back into his father's home after years of running up debts and living the high life. This caused his hardworking brother much envy and chagrin. The unconditional love and forgiveness of the father for the wayward son is similar to the unconditional love of God for you. A love that is given freely, regardless of anything you may have done. What matters most is that you are honest with God about who you really are.

What can occur after completing Step Five? The twelfth-century Cistercian monk Bernard of Clairveaux notes that a spiritual journey involves listening to what is in our hearts:

Only by the movement of my heart ... did I
recognise His presence ... and I came to wonder
at the depth of His wisdom.[24]

Julian of Norwich, the fourteenth-century nun who lived as an anchoress attached to a church in Norwich,

England, left us with many beautiful and uplifting spiritual writings. She also gave solace to those who passed by her cell, often giving out insightful spiritual guidance. Her message is clear: self-knowledge can open you up to God:

> We can never come to the full knowledge of God
> until we first clearly know our own soul.
> until the time that it is in its full powers,
> we cannot be all holy ...
> Our passing life that we have
> here does not know in our senses what our self is,
> but we know in our faith.
> And when we know and see, truly and clearly,
> what our self is, then we shall know truly and
> clearly see and know our
> Lord God in the fullness of joy.[25]

CHAPTER SIX

OPENNESS

Step Six : Were entirely ready to have God remove all
these defects of character.

*We must know that God regards our purity of heart
and tears of compunction, not our many words.*
(The Rule of Benedict, 20.3)[1]

DAVID'S STORY

Seeing a therapist helped me sort out what were my issues and what were the issues of other people — what I needed to let go of and what I needed to aim for. Often I realised that my perceptions of people and events were distorted, that I was often overcome with feelings of resentment and paranoia, particularly regarding what other people thought of me. Self-centredness was rearing its ugly head.

I still needed to address where I had acted out of rage and hurt other people. I realised that often my own shame had been projected onto other people in those circumstances.

I needed to be prepared to sort out what were natural responses to the abusive behaviour of others, and acknowledge where I was hurt or angered by that behaviour. Once I had tried to address that, then I could move on. I also learnt to be careful not to suppress anger, but acknowledge it and grow beyond it, to work through it and not be dictated to by it, in other words. I realised that suppressing anger could be a self-destructive thing.

Acknowledging anger along with my fear and resentments helped free me from my bonds.

~~~

In these next two steps you are addressing all in your experience that advances or hinders the soul in its quest for God. Both Steps Six and Seven centre around humility: being entirely ready and humble in spirit to allow God to remove whatever separates you from Him/Her. A key issue with this step is willingness. Again this requires humility and honesty. A Twelve Step program catchcry is 'honesty, open-mindedness and willingness'. As Bill W writes:

> *Let us never fear needed change …*
> *The essence of all growth is a willingness*
> *to change for the better*
> *and then an unremitting*
> *willingness to shoulder whatever*
> *responsibility this entails.*[2]

Letting go leads to forgiveness. There needs to be a willingness to let go of past fear and hurts in the process of doing Step Six. It is important to remember you are moving towards wholeness, not perfection. For example, as well as self-centredness, the inability to forgive yourself may be a defect of character, as is believing one is a failure instead of a divine creation by God.

However earnestly you embark on this process, some of these 'wounds' may never be removed; perhaps they will only be lessened in their intensity and capacity to overpower you. Because your gifts come from God, it is also spiritually enhancing at this stage to acknowledge attributes as well as defects.

SACRED WOUNDS

There is a paradox in facing these powerful character traits that confront you. Some of these 'wounds' or hurts, such as a volatile nature, may stay with you but no longer dominate you to the same degree. Learning to live with and accept inherent flaws is part of the nature of a healing journey.

The Franciscan spiritual writer Richard Rohr observes that there are three major things that undermine spirituality — the desire for power, prestige and position.[3] Often these things may have driven your life, and searching for them caused enormous distress.

Much of this is connected to sacred wounds according to Rohr. As with David's story, these wounds may have been 'natural responses to the abusive behaviour of others'. They may be wounds involving parents or other significant relationships or the legacy of severe emotional, sexual or physical abuse. You cannot fix these wounds by yourself or control your woundedness. It is what you do with those wounds, how you grow beyond them and how you incorporate them into yourself that will affect your spiritual growth.

A FREEDOM FOR GOD

David realised that his perceptions of the world were distorted. Such realisations, which you may experience with Steps Six and Seven, may also help you create a freedom for God. A freedom for God involves the integration of decisions, choices, prayer and action as you grow into a conscious choice for God, Christ or your Higher Power. Many of those healed by Christ embody this message in the New Testament. The gospel stories of the blind seeing again reflect this integration. For example, Bartimaeus, acknowledging Jesus as Lord and Master, asks him, '"Let me see again." Jesus replied, "Go; your faith has saved you". At once Bartimaeus' sight returned and he followed Jesus along the road' (Mark 10:51,52). So it is with you. A readiness to allow God to remove what separates you from Him/Her can open up your sight to see what you need to let go of.

Another biblical story along this theme of being released is the resurrection of Lazarus in John's Gospel. This is partly a story about resurrection and the recognition of Jesus as the Son of God and it is also a story about being set free of the ties that bind. When Jesus calls for the dead man Lazarus to 'come out!', he comes out of the tomb with his feet and hands bound. It is then that Jesus calls on the crowd to 'unbind him, let him go free' (John 11:43–44).

This story provides another way of understanding the Christian concept of triumph over death. Lazarus is also coming back from a spiritual place. In relating this to your own situation, how can you respond to Jesus' calls to Lazarus to 'be unbound and set free'? David's acknowledgment and understanding of his anger helped free him of its hold on him. He was able to cut the ties. Perhaps God is calling you back from the places where you don't belong, from those things that keep you in a state of 'death'.

When you undertake the next two steps concerning character defects you are desiring that God set you free, that God unbind you from the things that hold you back. Again the emphasis is on desire and willingness, not action.

As with the previous steps, you must undergo this process at your own pace and capacity. Some of your defects may be hard to let go of and may never be relinquished, for example, egoism and fear. Fear can sometimes be equated with a powerful state of desolation or a stifling character trait that can dramatically distort your perceptions of the world.

DEVELOPING DISCERNMENT:
STEP SIX WITH ST IGNATIUS

For those who are 'entirely ready' to start on this step there may be a desire for deeper reflection. If you want to address this step in a more intense way, St Ignatius offers powerful tools of prayer and reflection for discernment and decision making.

Discernment is crucial in this step as your choices affect your spiritual life. David was able to grow in understanding of what his issues were and what the issues of others were. This helped him work out what he needed to let go of and strive for. Becoming willing for God to remove defects of character or traits that have held you back in life means you need to be particular about what needs to be removed. This requires openness and receptiveness to the movements of your heart and to identify which characteristics are from God and which are not from God.

You can begin this step by saying a preparatory prayer from the first week of the Ignatian exercises. You ask for grace from God that all your daily life, intentions and actions be fully oriented towards worship and service of God ...[4]

You are dealing with the movements of your heart and the movements of your soul that affect your interior life. Sometimes these movements may be a blatant move away from God and at other times they may be more subtle. In helping to discern these movements you need to ask what aspects of your nature lead to consolation or an openness and love of God and what leads to a move away from God, to desolation or to the darkness of the soul.[5]

Good and evil spirits come from within your very self, outside of you, or from others.[6] Evil spirits can be considered as those subtle things that undermine your self-worth, things that make you feel unlovable or a failure, those movements of heart and spirit that seek to separate you from your dependence on a Higher Power.

For those undergoing the 'soul cleansing' that happens with Steps Six and Seven, 'it is the way of the evil spirit', says Ignatius, 'to bite, sadden and put obstacles, disquieting with false reasons that one may not go on', while consolations bring a greater sense of courage and strength.[7] This is where you need to gradually develop discernment as you might experience a mixture of these feelings as you undergo these steps.

To embrace the will of God is to enter fully into the human experience. This is akin to experiencing the passion of Jesus Christ shown in the third week of the Ignatian exercises. Feelings of compassion or distress may accompany this process[8] because you are dealing with powerful aspects of your humanity that have driven your life.

Remember there is a resurrection. In the fourth week God utterly consoles the soul and fills it with joy and light.

After his trouble with the powers of the day Jesus could have chosen the easier, softer way and escaped into the desert. He chose to go back to Jerusalem and face his inevitable horror-filled crucifixion. The biggest temptation for Jesus and for most of us on Steps Six and Seven is probably the desire to return to the safe and the familiar. This is the big temptation: to stay with character traits that keep you bound up in old behaviours that no longer serve you and leave you, like David, constantly overcome with feelings such as resentment and paranoia.

In Step Six you look with humility and discernment at those characteristics that may have caused you immense pain and hardship. You recognise that these defects or shortcomings are still with you and acknowledge your readiness to let them go and to move away from something that was once a familiar way of being.

CHAPTER SEVEN
The New Self Begins To Emerge

Step Seven: Humbly asked him to
remove our shortcomings.

*O Lord, you were turning me around to look at
myself. For I had placed myself behind my own
back, refusing to see myself ... you brought me face
to face with myself once more ...*
(*St Augustine*)[1]

CHRISTINE'S STORY

Fear and I have been very good companions for many years. I often wonder what my life would be like without it. Probably peaceful, trusting, exciting and embracing. Most aspects of my life are rolling along nicely; I have a great husband who adores me, children who I adore, a nice home. So what have I got to be fearful about? The truth is I am afraid of my passion. I am afraid I will not be successful.

I am a writer. I believe the gift of writing has come to me through God. I am afraid, I procrastinate, I sidetrack, I put others in front of my passion, I constantly seek approval. I guess you would call this list my shortcomings and they all stem from fear.

So how do I deal with this fear? I acknowledge I am truly human and am doing my best. I ask for help and then I hang on. Trust, faith, patience and humility are all required when one surrenders, and perhaps a steady acceptance of the fact that I am powerless over my fear. I am also willing to feel the fear about my passion and trust that I can write and learn to be patient with the process.

Humbly asking God for help is the last thing I try. I find it difficult to surrender and get out of the way. I tell myself that things won't happen for me.

~

The nature of Step Seven is that you have come to a point where you humbly ask God to free you from specific character defects or obsessive attachments that separate you from spiritual and inner freedom. This is a continual lifelong process and you might find yourself coming back to this step regularly.

Recognising your own frailties will enable you to become closer to the reality of yourself. While pain may be the price you pay for this insight, the blessing is the measure of humility. This blessing can heal the pain[2] as it has enabled you to move out from yourself and to let go of self, as well as becoming more focused and closer to God.

On beginning Step Seven you might reflect that:

> If we still cling to something we will not let go, we
> ask God to help us be willing. When ready, we say
> something like this: 'My Creator, I am now willing
> that you should have all of me, good and bad. I pray
> that you now remove from me every single defect of
> character, which stands in the way of my usefulness
> to you and my fellows. Grant me strength, as I go out
> from here, to do your bidding. Amen.'[3]

As Christine's story shows, in this process of moral inventory in Step Seven you are reminded of some aspects of your humanity that seek to dominate you and can become things that hold you back. These can include pride, fear, shame and lust. Pride is a big one because it can stifle your willingness to reach out to God or to others.

Because it is taken in humility this step can help you let go of false pride which deludes you into thinking you must stay in control and not let others know what is in your heart. Owning your flaws can turn them into assets, helping you to learn and grow from them. Your failures and vulnerabilities can become tools of inner knowledge that you can help yourself and help others with. 'Humility is strength', or as the Gospel says, 'the last will be first and the first will be last' (Matthew 20:16), and 'Anyone who loses his life for my sake will find it' (Matthew 10:39).

A great message for those on a spiritual path is not to see yourself as having conquered your shortcomings, but rather to accept that only God has the capacity to relieve these burdens. This acceptance puts you in a position of great spiritual strength. By the very path you have chosen you no longer worship the illusion of personal power, which has brought destruction in one form or another or is, at the very least, finite.

It is also important to remember that asking God to remove these shortcomings may mean they will be removed in God's timeframe, not yours. The following reflections of St Ignatius and St Augustine bear this out.

Acknowledging that you are truly human and are doing your best, like Christine, can help complete this step. You need to accept that you will probably take many character flaws with you to the grave.

Understanding that ultimately you know nothing is another key to spiritual wisdom. Step Seven might involve trusting in God to reveal what you need to let go of, and also what you may live with as a part of your own woundedness. That sacred wound may indeed be transformed into an asset. The monk John Cassian advises:

> *For he is next door to understanding*
> *who carefully recognises*
> *what he ought to ask about,*
> *nor is he far from knowledge*
> *who begins to understand how ignorant he is.*[4]

GROWING IN FREEDOM WITH IGNATIUS

As it is in this step, the point of the Ignatian exercises is to grow in freedom and to attend to God's spirit moving in you. The attainment of true spiritual freedom, according to Ignatius, comes about by bringing an order of values into your life. Out of that order of values you can make choices and decisions free from the influence of any obsessive attachment.

Often you focus on everything else in your life except the thing you most need to: opening your heart to God. Instead you may even pray harder or work harder rather than face the particular attachment.[5] It is in such circumstances that you may often find you need to humbly ask for shortcomings to be removed. This is to help diffuse or let go of the attachment. For example, you may have a way of avoiding looking at your own fears and resentments in your relationships by obsessively helping others. In the guise of this good act you might be doing yourself harm. By failing to attend to the needs of your closest relationship you harm it.

In Christine's story, her fear of failure often stopped her growing as a person. You might then ask yourself, where have I missed the mark in my own life? Where did I miss opportunities for growth or self-fulfilment because of my own nature? How can I overcome this?

ST AUGUSTINE'S SPIRITUAL LEGACY

One of the giants of Western Christendom was St Augustine, who eventually held a powerful position as Bishop of Hippo (in Africa) towards the end of the fourth century. Many of the difficulties Augustine struggled with in his famous pilgrimage of conversion are not that dissimilar to your own.

His spirituality was a 'mysticism of action'. He saw no

conflict between a life of contemplation and a life of action. He sought intimacy with God but also lived very much in the world. He was a person who experienced a gradual journey of conversion after many years of being a womaniser and a pleasure seeker. Augustine believed that conversion to faith comes about through God's grace manifesting itself in us. You allow for this openness to grace, which is a gift, and then all the joys which come into your life come from God.

Augustine's story has a great message. It is testimony to the fact that there is no greater miracle than faith and inner transformation brought about by owning up to who you really are.

Augustine's famous treatise, *Confessions*, captures the emotional, passionate and moving encounter between the human soul that hungers for intimacy with God and the flawed human condition, manifesting itself as a conflict between 'Truth' and the life of 'habit', inner conflict and worldly pursuits, and the struggle with intention.

This is applicable to the practice of Step Seven. Much of what Augustine struggled with concerned the conflict between what might be termed today as self-will and God's will: the struggle with human nature on the one hand, and the call to be with God on the other.

Augustine believed he was in the chains of his obsessions and compulsions. His conversion was slow but intense. Through contemporary eyes you may not identify with his famous struggle in seeking to renounce his relationships with women, but as you come back to Step Seven regularly, you can look at his struggle in relation to the shortcomings that dominate your own life. Asking God to remove the emptiness you often encounter when you look for material things outside yourself to satisfy you is just one example of this.

Occasional despair, frustration or distance from God are inevitable stumbling blocks on the path of a serious spiritual journey. Augustine desired spiritual fulfilment but feared it might mean losing what was familiar and comfortable to him.

He knew only too well the struggle you can often have with intentions and how you deceive yourself with your motives. For example, Christine's seeking of approval was more from fear of rejection. Augustine reminds us that:

The appearance of what we do is often different
from the intention with which we do it,
and the circumstances at the time may not be clear.[6]

All of your experiences, both good and bad, can teach you something. Despite his mystical experiences and epiphanies along the way, Augustine all too readily fell back into his old behaviour and it took time before he was fully converted. Yet these experiences did not leave him untouched by the presence of God.

It is no surprise that Augustine, who would have been familiar with the life of the famous desert monk St Antony, eventually came to understand that it is in the innermost call of your heart that you can listen to God and ultimately find God:

> O God, hope of my youth, where were you all this
> time? Where were you hiding from me ...Yet I was
> walking on a treacherous path, in darkness. I was
> looking for you outside myself, and I did not find
> the God of my own heart.[7]

Augustine's struggles ultimately brought him face to face with his own fragility. This is also your task: to allow yourself to be at a point where you are naked before your true self and conscience.

Augustine found out through his own searching that many of our learnt behaviours are hard to relinquish. For,

> ... while Truth teaches it [the soul]
> to prefer one course,
> habit prevents it from relinquishing the other ...
> this was the nature of my sickness.
> I was in torment ...
> And you, O lord, never ceased to
> watch over my secret heart ...[8]

Like many of the Desert Fathers and Mothers, Augustine's eventual conversion brought him the gift of tears:

> *I probed the hidden depths of my soul and*
> *wrung its pitiful secrets from it,*
> *and when I mustered them all*
> *before the eyes of my heart,*
> *a great storm broke within me,*
> *bringing with it a great deluge of tears.*[9]

Augustine's contribution for the purpose of completing the steps of moral inventory may well be his understanding of the role of God's grace and mercy in a person's life:

> *Where else, then, did I find you, to learn of you,*
> *unless it was in yourself, above me?*
> *Whether we approach you or depart from you,*
> *you are not confined in any place. You are Truth,*
> *and you are everywhere present where all seek*
> *counsel of you … The [one] who serves you best is*
> *the one who is less intent on hearing from you*
> *what he wills to hear than on shaping his will*
> *according to what he hears from you.*[10]

He knew that despite the uncertainty many face on a spiritual journey, 'the only firm promise we have is your mercy'.[11] So 'cast yourself upon God and have no fear'.[12]

CHAPTER EIGHT

OWNING UP TO THE PAST

Step Eight: Made a list of all persons we had harmed and became willing to make amends to them all.

> *Some wrongs we can never fully right.*
> (*Alcoholics Anonymous*)[1]

JENNIFER'S STORY

I made the list. I became willing. But I didn't even realise I had been hurting him, causing him harm for such a long, long time. We always seemed to argue about everything. I loved him. He was my husband. We even got married again after ten years. But you know the saying: 'We harm the ones we love the most'.

One day, we were arguing about the year ahead. He said, 'I won't do my university law course this year so you can start up your business'. I said, 'You're only saying that to make me feel guilty … There is no way you would really want to give up your dream to let me do mine.'

What I didn't realise in the heat of the moment was that he really did mean it. He loved me so much, he wanted to see me run my own business. He knew that it was really important to me. He also knew that for us being a working couple, and bringing up small children, something had to give and he was the one prepared to let go of something.

Identifying the harm done was probably the most

difficult. I tried to make him feel bad about letting go of his uni course. We went to bed not talking. It was not until the next day that I realised what I had done and that I had been doing it for a long time. I was not accepting his unconditional love. I believe this was because I didn't believe anyone could love me that much. Through reflection using this step I realised I harm those who try to love me. I feel that they want something in return from me, or that they are insincere, so I find it difficult to accept love.

This experience also started me thinking that Christ loves me unconditionally and wants the best for me. I've been a Christian for seventeen years. But it took me this long to accept what that really means, to be loved unconditionally.

$$\longrightarrow$$

All of us forgive in different ways and have different types of wounds that we carry. Forgiveness is also about becoming free of the wounds we hold on to. The blessing is it can bring us freedom and distance from a situation that may have troubled us for a long time, not to mention the long yearned for relief and peace of mind.

These next two steps, the eighth and ninth, are about looking at all areas of your life, your relationships in particular, and becoming willing to set things right; to make amends to people you have harmed. It is aimed at repairing past wrongs and freeing yourself of guilt, so that you can live in peace. This frees you to become more connected to yourself and other people.

To start to make amends may mean a willingness to undertake a gentle exercise in reparation for something you have done or a token act of penance. On the other hand, it may involve making a generous gesture towards someone you have harmed or an apology along with a humble and honest explanation for your past behaviour.

You may never do these steps fully, but what matters is that you do them to the best of your ability as issues arise. There may be some wrongs that you can never right, but this is where acceptance comes in. Above all, you need to forgive yourself. This can often be the hardest part.

Making a list of the people, debts or situations which obviously appear as priorities for reparation is a start. This is the way you begin to 'straighten out the past'. As with other steps, you may come back to Steps Eight and Nine regularly, but the willingness is what counts.

Remember you are experiencing a 'death' of self in these steps, so you need to pray for direction. In regards to your attitudes to those who have harmed you, it is also wise to reflect on the reasons why you feel the way you do and seek spiritual guidance. Prayer is not only a way you can forgive, but also a way of discerning where you need to practise forgiveness.

If you are unsure, you can also ask God to direct you to those people to whom you should make amends. You may not be able to locate all you have harmed or remember who you have harmed in your life, but what you can do is pray for willingness to make amends where appropriate.

So you do not get caught up in over-scrupulous or unnecessary guilt, it is probably wise to listen to your heart. It has the answer. As Scripture says: 'Not every kind of shame is right to harbour, nor is every situation correctly appraised by all' (Ecclesiastes 41:16).

To start working on owning up to your past in Steps Eight and Nine, humility, poverty of spirit and a willingness to be led where you need to be led will guide you. All you can do is trust.

CHAPTER NINE
MAKING UP FOR THE PAST

Step Nine: Made direct amends to such people where possible except when to do so would injure them or others.

The Lord waits for us daily to translate into action, as we should, his holy teachings. Therefore our life span has been lengthened by a way of a truce, that we may amend our misdeeds.
(The Rule of Benedict: Prologue)[1]

CAROL'S STORY

The Steps for me are a way to God and freedom. They are my lifeline, my strength. It's two in the morning and I arrive at the AA Central Service Office in Los Angeles, California. I am on a faith journey to the United States, practising Step Three, abandoning myself to God. It is my fourth sober birthday and I want to welcome the day in gratitude. So I offer to answer the phones in the early hours of this Friday.

I notice an amends letter to my brother poking out of my journal. I had no intention of bringing it and all of a sudden I am dialing his number in Australia. It's Friday night there, he's at home and I find myself asking him if it is a good time, if he is willing to listen to an amends letter I have written to him. I explain it's part of my program and he says, 'Of course'.

I read him the letter, word for word. At the time I wrote it, I had no intention of actually reading it to him. I finish and wait. He thanks me and says how beautiful it is, and that he is touched and it is the best thing that has happened to him all week.

After I hang up I sit back in my chair and look around the office. At that moment gratitude fills my soul and every cell in my body. Sometimes there are not enough words for it. A warm feeling washes over me. I feel incredibly close to God.

Step Nine is my first major experience that the steps are working in my life. I am a long way from the terrified, insane, drug-and-alcohol-dependent girl that crawled into these rooms. I say a prayer of thanks to God for my sobriety, for my life, and for the relationship with my brother.

Much of the work of this step involves letting go of the ego, turning away from yourself to look out on the world. As Carol's story shows, it is very much about fronting up to things you have done or failed to do and being accountable. Your humility is your strength.

RECONCILIATION AND ATONEMENT: THE RESPONSE OF LOVE

Confession, now called reconciliation, is the traditional sacrament of penance in the Catholic Church. Many people undergo this sacramental rite because intuitively they know that 'the truth will set them free'.

The idea of penance in the history of Christianity was to make reparation for past moral failures. Today you can see it as involving deep sorrow for what you have done[2] and having a firm desire to make things right and to devote yourself more readily to God.[3] You desire to make up for what you have done, and accept whatever consequences come with that intention. Remember Jesus' words: 'I have come to call not the upright but sinners to repentance' (Luke 5:32).

This act of reconciliation is a sacramental encounter, which gives a whole new sense of meaning and acknowledges that Christ is truly present.[4] The Benedictine John Main writes:

Every sacramental reality
is a celebration of the reality of the presence of
Christ united to our human spirit,
praying to the Father in our human heart.[5]

This sacramental reality can be a healing and bonding act and it can lead to greater intimacy with God. Reconciliation can free you up to be more open to love and to become more forgiving of others. The same applies to the act of penance or making amends. In whatever form it takes, it can be viewed as a love response to God involving movements of the heart. This is what you attempt to do to the best of your ability with Steps Eight and Nine.

In the Christian biblical tradition, the time of Jubilee (the year 2000 was such a year) was ideally a time when debts were wiped, slaves freed and alienated land was returned to ancestral owners. In the Old Testament passage, God speaks to Moses on Mt Sinai instructing him on the year of Jubilee, telling him it will be:

> *... a holy thing for you ...*
> *each of you will return to his ancestral property.*
> *If you buy land from, or sell land to, your fellow*
> *countryman, neither of you may exploit the other ...*
> *fear your God, for I am Yahweh your God.*
> *(Leviticus 25:8–17)*

The Jubilee occurred every fifty years and was aimed towards liberating the oppressed and bringing about atonement and redemption. It would begin on the Day of Atonement, a Jewish feast where the community ritually atoned for its sins. Symbolically and actively it was a time for reconciliation, a time to make things right.

This same principle can be applied to the idea of reconciliation in your own spiritual journey. You can be reconciled by making things right and by becoming willing to clear debts and attempting to repair damaged relationships.

Prayer is a journey to the centre of your being, and it also has the power to release you from the burden of self-obsession and bring you closer to God. Once you are more connected to the Other, whether it be by prayer, ritual, sacrament or sharing your stories, you can reconnect with other people. Compassion for self will lead to compassion for others.

THE PURPOSE OF RELIGION

The true purpose of religion should be to reconnect people with the Other. The Latin root of 'religion' suggests a relinking or reconnection.[6] The Franciscan Richard Rohr observes that all great religion, all healthy religion, is about what you do with your pain and how you transform it to come out the other side resurrected.[7]

This is part of what you are doing with this step. John Main writes:

> *The Lord, as we know, purifies those who draw*
> *near to him in a growing consciousness*
> *of his supreme reality.*
> *The roots of our egoism are dried up by*
> *the work of love that is our prayer.*
> *And as we turn more openly to the Spirit,*
> *in our inmost being,*
> *so does the phantom of the ego gradually disappear.*[8]

Humility deepens and nurtures the spiritual life, yet it is often overtaken by the ego. Feeding the Twelve Steps and this step in particular are humility and charity. To quote one of the Desert Fathers:

> *If you see [someone] pure and humble,*
> *that is a great vision.*
> *For what is greater than such a vision,*
> *to see the invisible God in a visible [person].*[9]

God means you to experience all of your humanity, including your own woundedness. As the beaten know only too well, those who open themselves to God, through emptiness and poverty of spirit, can sometimes experience God more intensely.

POVERTY OF SPIRIT

St Benedict also knew that poverty of spirit is the pathway to God and freedom. It brings life. For those who need to make amends, though your past behaviour may have held you back, caused you and others harm, or brought you 'death', you can now move into 'life':

> *As the Apostle says:*
> *Do you not know that the patience of God*
> *is leading you to repent? (Romans 2:4)*

And indeed the Lord assures us in his love:
I do not wish the death of the sinner,
but that he turn back to me and live.
(Ezekiel 33:11)[10]

When you face another human being and make amends, whether or not you are forgiven by that person, you can face the presence of God.

The poverty of spirit embodied by the mystics is what you aim for in the spiritual life. Your poverty of spirit, often experienced through your own flaws, becomes an asset. Bill W knew this only too well in relation to his experience of alcoholism:

So it is necessary for all of us to accept
whatever positive gifts we receive
with a deep humility, always bearing in
mind that our negative attitudes
were first necessary as a means of reducing
us to such a state that we would
be ready for a gift of the positive ones
via the conversion experience.
Your own alcoholism and the immense
deflation that finally resulted are indeed the
foundation upon which
your spiritual experience rests.[11]

This step can bring about a great feeling of gratitude, and can make you feel closer to God. It can also bring about a feeling of being forgiven and a real sense of letting go of the past with its all-pervading sense of alienation and abandonment.

CHAPTER TEN
CONTINUAL TRANSFORMATION AND FREEDOM
FROM THE BONDAGE OF SELF

Step Ten: Continued to take personal inventory and when we were wrong promptly admitted it.

Oh search me God and know my heart ...
(Psalm 139:23)

JANE'S STORY

It is sometimes difficult to take responsibility, or even be able to see with any clarity what has actually occurred in an unpleasant situation. It is much easier to take the high moral ground and blame others. Sometimes special spiritual friends can inspire great gifts to come from otherwise dark situations. I was lucky to have such a friend. His name was Bill.

My early recovery from active alcoholism was a bewildering and fearful time. Every area of my life was in tatters. I heard a saying that 'life lived as a means to an end is self-robbery'. I was bankrupt in all areas of my life.

It was suggested that as soon as I was physically well I should get a job to support my son and pay off my debts. I was also looking after my grandfather. Although it was very tiring, I started to feel better about myself. Grandfather died and this left me lonely and quite bereft. Two years later my mother died and my grief compounded. This meant I became quite well off financially so I stopped work and started university.

At this stage a woman, who appeared very consoling and helpful, befriended me. After a while she suggested that I finance her in part ownership of a house. I later realised the old saying, 'a fool and their money are soon parted'. The house went; the money went. On top of all that, my son's life was falling apart and I was trying to finish an honours degree. My life was again in chaos and my heart was filled with resentment.

When I talked with Bill I was extremely angry and self-righteous. He cut me short and said, 'If you want to learn anything from this experience then ask yourself, "Why was I there, what did I expect to gain from this situation?"' He said that if I could see my own part in the situation, then I would find out how I had compromised myself subconsciously.

~~~~

Step Ten is about bringing together all that you have learnt from Steps Four to Nine into your daily life. It can be experienced with increasing clarity and insight, as Jane's story shows. By looking honestly at her part in being exploited she was able to grow.

Allowing for the gradual healing of negative and destructive patterns is part of acceptance and of adhering to the Twelve Step philosophy of growing along spiritual lines, rather than aiming for spiritual perfection. Praying for insight into why you do what you do, accepting it and praying for it to be released is a start.

Practising forgiveness of yourself and others is also part of this process. God is always able to forgive, regardless of what you do wrong in life. The great stories of scripture such as the Prodigal Son (Luke 15:11–32), the woman caught in adultery (John 8:1–11), the woman who wept over Jesus' feet at the house of Simon the Pharisee (Luke 7:36–50) and the treatise on 'love your enemies' (Luke 6:27–36) remind us of this forgiveness.

THE IMPORTANCE OF SELF-KNOWLEDGE

As Jane's story demonstrates, to continue to take personal inventory is not 'giving yourself a hard time' or looking for defects. Rather it is recognising where certain behaviours interrupt the flow of your life or keep you from the knowledge that you are truly loved by God. This is an important point. The woman at Jesus' feet was forgiven because she had shown such great love (Luke 7:44–49).

Self-knowledge helps to liberate you. The core things that used to motivate and drive you no longer dominate or control you to the same degree. For:

We have entered the world of Spirit.
Our next function is to grow in understanding
and effectiveness.

This is not an overnight matter.
It should continue for our lifetime.
Continue to watch for selfishness, dishonesty,
resentment, and fear.[1]

Happiness or contentment are often by-products of setting things right as you go along. The blessing of greater spiritual awareness gives you the ability to look at the things that bring you closer to God and those that distance you from God. You may also realise that much peace of mind comes from acceptance and gratitude. This is the key to Step Ten.

An honest regret for harms done, a genuine
gratitude for blessings received,
and a willingness to try for better things tomorrow
will be the permanent assets we shall seek ...
having searched our hearts with neither
fear nor favor, we can truly thank God
for the blessings we have received and
sleep in good conscience.[2]

THE PSALMS:
GOD IS ALWAYS PRESENT

If you do not know what you need to take account of in your life or you have reached a block, pray for guidance. Many of the Davidic psalms in the Old Testament can offer comfort. They reflect a passionate faith relationship with God amid the highs and lows of life and illustrate the struggles that are implicit in an uncertain world. These psalms are attributed to David and they show that despite his struggles, David eventually became King of Israel. The psalms are a reminder that God has a plan for your life, even though that plan may be a mystery:

> *How hard for me to grasp your thoughts,*
> *How many, God there are!*
> *If I count them, they are more than the grains of sand;*
> *If I come to an end, I am still with you ...*
> *God, examine me and know my heart,*
> *Test me and know my concerns.*
> *Make sure that I am not on my way to ruin,*
> *And guide me on the road of eternity.*
> *(Psalm 139:17–18; 23–24)*

CONTINUING TO SEARCH YOUR SOUL WITH IGNATIUS

Ignatian tools of discernment and decision making help you to do Step Ten, especially in working out where consolation and desolation are happening in your life.[3]

> *Beware of thinking to yourself,*
> *'My own strength and the might of my*
> *own hand have given me the power to act like this.'*
> *Remember Yahweh your God; he was the one who*
> *gave you the strength to act effectively like*
> *this, thus keeping then, as today, the covenant which*
> *he swore to your ancestors.*
> *(Deuteronomy 8:17,18)*

Ignatian spirituality emphasises that if you know your own weaknesses you know how you can lose the way. In contemporary understanding this means that you need to be aware of subtle impulses that are actually self-destructive. The 'evil spirits' St Ignatius referred to are not 'evil' as we currently understand it; rather, they are emotions or personal drives that can influence our behaviour and lead us away from God. Like a false lover the 'evil spirit' knows your weaknesses and can capitalise on them.[4]

For example, Jane's situation may have revealed to her that she had an excessive need to be needed. Another example of this might be when you begin to love someone and get close to them but you are fearful of rejection. Your low self-esteem is an internal voice telling you that you are worthless or don't deserve love. Such subtle feelings can be potentially destructive.

ST BENEDICT AND THE IMPORTANCE OF A BALANCED LIFE

Despite its origins in a world of social chaos, barbarian invasion and political uncertainty not unlike much of our own postmodern world, the Rule of Benedict explained the need to aim for balance in life. It did not advocate extreme asceticism, but focused on the life of Christ within the individual. Much like the mystical writers, the Rule emphasised singleness of heart in seeking only God and the spiritual bliss that comes through unceasing charity and prayer.

WORKING AGAINST THE ALIENATED SELF

When you are working towards a greater balance and acceptance in your life, you need to remind yourself that there are times when, despite your willingness, you cannot escape from entrenched negative and self-destructive patterns of behaviour that have been part of your psyche for a long time.

What is traditionally known in Christian thought as 'sin' or bad behaviour can be seen as alienation from your centre. This really means disconnection or fragmentation from your loving self. Benedictine John Main describes this as:

> ... *self-centredness,*
> *being locked into one's self as a monad,*
> *and living the nightmare of finding only distorted*
> *images of this illusion wherever one looks, and in*
> *whomsoever one meets.*[5]

Continual conversion, *metanoia*, helps liberate and summon you from this state, through being focused on things outside yourself which help lead you to God. This means that you are continually keeping track or taking a personal inventory of your faults that hold you back from moving on to discover different aspects of your life.

JULIAN OF NORWICH: WE NEED TO FALL

In 1373, a mystic and anchoress of great influence, Julian of Norwich, experienced her 'Showings' where visually, emotionally and spiritually she witnessed the Passion of Christ. Before this spiritual revelation she prayed to experience the wounds of contrition, compassion and longing for God.[6]

In her cell next to a church in Norwich, England, many people would come to her window to seek advice and spiritual guidance on all manner of problems. Her writings are a continual reminder that God's love is present regardless of what you do, and that sometimes, like Jane, you need to see certain things about yourself, and it may take adversity or a bad situation to help reveal them:

> *We need to fall, and we need to see it; for if we did*
> *not fall, we should not know how feeble and how*
> *wretched we are in ourselves,*
> *nor, too, should we know so completely the*
> *wonderful love of our Creator.*[7]

Throughout her writings Julian of Norwich emphasises this great insight — that although suffering and the adversity brought on by human behaviour will always occur in life, these states are temporary and ultimately all will be well. Long after her famous visions of the Passion of Christ had stopped, Julian offered these famous words to reassure those who continually fall into negative patterns so that they need not despair:

Often I wondered why [in] the great
foreseeing wisdom of God
the beginning of sin was not letted ...
And our Lord answered:
Sin is behovable [inevitable], but all shall be well,
and all shall be well
and all manner of things shall be well.[8]

You may suffer and get caught up in your faults but this is temporary and blessings can follow:

... and it seems to me that this pain is
something for a time, for it
purges us and makes us know ourselves
and ask for mercy; for the
Passion of our Lord is comfort to us against all this,
and that is his blessed will for all who will be saved.
He comforts readily and sweetly with his words,
and says: But all will be well, and every kind
of thing will be well.[9]

CHAPTER ELEVEN
CONTINUING ON THE JOURNEY

Step Eleven: Sought through prayer and meditation to improve our conscious contact with God as we understood him, praying only for knowledge of his will for us and the power to carry that out.

> *But my friends should know truly*
> *That the more I draw them,*
> *The nearer they come to me.*
> *When [a person] makes a conquest over self,*
> *So that suffering and consolation weigh equally,*
> *Then will I raise him to blessedness*
> *And let him taste eternal life.*[1]

THERESE'S STORY

Practising Step Eleven is the key to a happy sobriety for me. It is a source of wisdom and a creative guide to right action and right thinking. It leads to a fuller, more abundant life, one not available without conscious contact with my Higher Power.

In the early days of my recovery, I held rigidly onto the God I heard about in meetings, praying fervently for another day's sobriety every morning and thanking God for that sobriety at the end of the day. God was a force for intervention in my life at that time. I believed God wanted change and total commitment from me. I would ask God to change this or that difficult situation, or this or that unacceptable thing in my personality.

At some point I came to believe that God wanted me to accept 'the hard thing', to enter the convent. I thought that this would prove my devotion. It was not what I wanted, but at the time I had a hard albeit loving God — one not of desire but of demands. A wise sponsor advised me to wait until I was five years sober before making that decision.

When my recovery became more of an everyday thing, I began to realise that God was not what I had thought. Sobriety came to be less about 'being good' than about 'being real'. God did not always answer my prayers in the ways or times I asked. I entered a period of darkness in my prayer life that I found very hard to understand. I would pray earnestly for help with some defect such as resentment or anger and find that it did not go away. The interventionist God gave way to a God of mysterious absence. The old sureties failed and my prayer life became dry and hard, like a desert walk to an unknown destination without a reliable guide.

More recently I have come back to a very simple form of prayer and meditation. Every morning, I spend between ten minutes to half an hour just making myself available to my Higher Power, breathing in and out and trying to let go of thoughts and embrace the presence of God.

Mostly, I just sit with my jumble and tumble of thoughts and try to bring my mind back to my breathing. While I rarely experience much serenity, I find that taking time to pray and meditate really makes a difference to my day. I often respond intuitively to difficult situations in ways I know would not have been available to me if I had not spent time with God in the morning. I see more beauty and more life around me. I am more open and relaxed with people.

Nowadays God is a mysterious presence in my life who

enables me to accept those parts of myself I cannot change. While much of my own shadow side is still part of my life, the difference is that now it matters less. God is part of the chaos as well as the creativity in my life, the unconscious as well as the conscious. Step Eleven has opened doors in my life I did not even dream were there.

LET GO AND LET GOD

As Therese's story shows us, prayer and meditation to a God or Higher Power of your own understanding enhances a sense of belonging and purposefulness. Praying only for God's will for you and the power to carry that out can also develop a greater acceptance that all will be well and result in you not getting so caught up in attachments or stressing out so much over the small things.

Therese's story also emphasises that there will be times in your life when you will revisit the desert experience, when your old self resurfaces or your faults temporarily take you over. That desert experience may also come to you in the form of emptiness, depression, desolation, or simply in a feeling of uncertainty or occasional distance from God. At times like these it is important to remember that sometimes in times of trouble or distress, God is calling for you to get closer.

Like Therese, moving through the Twelve Steps has

given you the resources to deal with those desert experiences. You may also come to realise that Step Eleven is as much about getting to know your real self and coming to love and accept that reality. Since you know that suffering is part of life, you seek to maintain constant contact with God through prayer and meditation, knowing that this is where peace and your 'freedom to be' lie, and where the answers will ultimately come.

TERESA OF AVILA: GOD IS YOUR FRIEND

Teresa of Avila, a friend and one time protégé of spiritual director St John of the Cross, like him advocated 'mental prayer', and saw mutual love, detachment and humility as the keystones of the spiritual life. For the down-to-earth Teresa, Jesus and God are your friends, and mental prayer means 'an intimate sharing between friends; it means taking time to be alone with Him who we know loves us'.[2] This is an approach that can easily be a good interpretation of Step Eleven and could take the form of writing, talking, conversational praying and so on.

PRAYER USING LECTIO DIVINA

In order to experience greater intimacy with God you need to believe, hope, love, and know your own emptiness. Another more intense and powerful form of prayer and meditation is the ancient wisdom of *lectio divina*, which is sometimes referred to as 'meditation', 'reading of the word' or 'holy reading'.

Meditation is part of all the great spiritual traditions. It is about seeking to empty the mind and heart of distractions, being still and allowing the Spirit to be present in you. It usually takes the form of sitting on a chair and breathing deeply for at least ten minutes, or ideally for about half an hour.

For those unfamiliar with meditation you can begin by simply setting aside twenty minutes in your day and repeating a mantra (a word or phrase) in your head. A good mantra is the Aramaic (the ancient Hebrew Jesus spoke) *maranatha* which means 'come, Lord, come'. You can use whatever mantra appeals to you so long as it is simple. You can also sit in silence with quiet meditative music in the background. In meditation you do not fight the intrusive thoughts or feelings that come and go, but learn to accept them, let them go and keep focusing on your mantra.

Lectio divina is profound, because it combines prayer and meditation. Prayer, where you speak to God saying words of homage or asking for guidance; and meditation, where you empty your mind of thoughts and continually recite a mantra.

Broken down into parts this prayer method is: *Lectio-Meditatio-Oratio-Contemplatio-Evangelizatio-Ruminatio*,[3] or 'read — understand — reflect — pray — be still — respond — continue to ponder'. In simpler terms this involves reading a short spiritual text and 'listening with the ear of your heart', understanding and reflecting on the text and considering how it might be applied in your life, then praying on your insights. Meditation using a mantra is often the easiest way to enter this part of *lectio divina*.

You might think about what God is calling for you to do and continue to think on a phrase from the text or message that has spoken to you throughout the rest of the day. The message may be as simple as, 'let go and let God'. This entire prayer process may take at least half an hour. This method of contemplation can be a powerful focus for your daily life, particularly for those times when you feel unsettled or stressed. It sums up Step Eleven using prayer and meditation to improve contact with God. It also helps to ground and enrich your spiritual life, your self-knowledge and your wisdom.

GREATER DISCERNMENT IN PRAYER THROUGH STEP ELEVEN

The famous St Ignatius prayer, part of the 'contemplation to gain love',[4] captures the essence of the Twelve Step program, especially Steps Three and Eleven:

Take, O Lord and receive
My entire liberty,
My memory, my understanding and my whole will.
All that I am and all that I possess
You have given me:
I surrender it all to You
To be disposed of according to Your will.
Give me only Your love and Your grace;
With these I will be rich enough,
And will desire nothing more.
(St Ignatius)[5]

Another way of implementing Step Eleven is to simply place yourself in the presence of God and ask God to direct your daily life in the way God wants, in a way that will serve God. In praying for what you want, you specifically ask 'for interior knowledge of great good received, in order that being entirely grateful, [we] may be able in all to love and serve [God]'.[6] You can leave the results of your prayer up to God. In the ups and downs of everyday life, God can bring about consolation without any necessary causes.[7] Grace can touch your life reassuring you of the relationship you share with God.

THE LOVER AND THE BELOVED

Crucially, the prayer relationship between you and God is similar to that of lovers. In Ignatian terms love consists 'in the lover giving and communicating to the beloved what he has or out of what he has'.[8] This intimacy, also known as love mysticism, is what you can strive for with this step, that is, a genuine relationship of giving and receiving between the beloved and the lover.

THE BEGUINES

The Beguines were a famous group of lay women who left a profound example of spiritual devotion. Their movement originated in Belgium in the late twelfth century and spread throughout Europe during the thirteenth century. The uniqueness of these women came from the way they blurred the boundaries between religious life and life in a lay community; they worked to earn a living while living devout lives. They did not take permanent vows, but would often move in and out of religious life. Their emphasis was on charity, humility and companionship.

The role of visions in the life of these women was profoundly illuminative and expressive of the new eucharistic devotion of the twelfth century, marked by an emphasis on the humanity and passion of Christ.

The mysticism of the visions of the Beguines was particularly personal, intimate, humane and feminine with an empathy for the ordinary person. This type of spirituality is extremely complementary to a Twelve Step journey. The Beguines did not shy away from pain or suffering, or the darkness or absence of God, and primarily focused on love as the ultimate expression of God.

JULIAN OF NORWICH: GOD COMFORTS US IN JOY AND SORROW

Julian of Norwich's example to the world also lies in her extraordinary compassion, her willingness to submit to the will of God, and her incredible appreciation of the role of God's grace, essential for those fulfilling this step of prayer and meditation: 'With all the will of my heart I assented wholly to be as was God's will',[9] she says, and '... our Lord showed me a spiritual sight of his familiar love. I saw that he is to us everything which is good and comforting for our help ...'[10]

The aim with this step is not self-depreciation, but is about emptying yourself for God, living with a broader connection to the world and putting your relationship with God first. Having let go of what you once knew and letting your soul continue on its journey towards union with God, you have become 'nothing for God':

For until I am substantially united to him I can
never have love or rest or true happiness;
until, that is, I am so attached to him that there can
be no created thing between my God and me.
And who will do this deed?
Truly, he himself, by his mercy and his grace,
for he has made me for this
and has blessedly restored me ...[11]

Not all times of prayer and meditation will leave you feeling connected to God or a Higher Power. Julian understood the need to be comforted by God in some instances and left to your own devices in others. Regarding those times in the spiritual desert where you do not necessarily feel any spiritual presence, Julian saw in her vision:

... that every [person] needs to experience this,
to be comforted at one time,
and at another to fail and to be left to [them]self.
God wishes us to know
that he keeps us safe all the time,
in joy and in sorrow, and that he loves
us as much in sorrow as in joy ...
Therefore, it is not God's will that when we feel
pain we should pursue it, sorrowing and mourning
for it, but that suddenly we should pass it over and
preserve ourselves in endless delight, because God is
almighty, our lover and preserver.[12]

Sometimes your difficulties in life may be part of God calling you in mysterious ways, the desire of God for you, the desire to be known. For God:

> *... wants us to accept our tarrying and our suffering*
> *as lightly as we are able,*
> *and to count them as nothing ... because of*
> *our love ... therefore if a [person] be in so much*
> *pain, so much woe, and so much unrest that*
> *it seems to him that he can think of nothing at*
> *all but the state he is in or what he is feeling,*
> *let him, as soon as he may, pass it over lightly*
> *and count it as nothing. Why? Because God*
> *wants to be known ...*[13]

FAITH, HOPE AND LOVE

To practise prayer and meditation you also need to remind yourself that without love you have no spiritual life. The love of God that changes and transforms someone is the epitome of the gift of self. God changes people who feel incapable of change. As Paul's famous passage from Corinthians reminds us:

> *And though I have the power of prophecy, to*
> *penetrate all mysteries and knowledge, and though I*
> *have all the faith necessary to move mountains — if I*

am without love, I am nothing. Though I should give
away to the poor all that I possess, and even give up
my body to be burned — if I am without love, it will
do me no good whatever ... Love never comes to an
end ... As it is, these remain: faith, hope and love, the
three of them; and the greatest of them is love.
(1 Corinthians 13:2–3; 8; 13)

FRANCIS OF ASSISI

Francis of Assisi, the famous saint and mystic of the early thirteenth century, knew only too well that praying in a state of humility was the pathway to God.

Francis had two life–changing experiences; the first was meeting and embracing a leper, and the second was when he received the call to serve God. His famous prayer embodies the spirit of Step Eleven and is an ideal prayer to say at the beginning of your day:

Most high
Glorious God,
Enlighten the darkness of my heart
And give me, Lord,
A correct faith,
A certain hope,
A perfect charity,
Sense and knowledge,

So that I may carry out Your holy
And true command.
Amen.

Francis came from a wealthy family and the meeting with the leper was probably very confronting for him. He might have felt the immense presence of God in the leper's suffering, the poverty of Christ or the emptiness and poverty of spirit in another human being. This event led to his conversion. He stripped naked before the local bishop and his father as a symbolic rejection of wealth and an adoption of poverty. It is said that his great experience of the poverty and humility of Christ made him the first recorded case of someone receiving the stigmata.

FREEDOM AND A PEACE THAT SURPASSES ALL UNDERSTANDING

Your goal in Step Eleven is to reach greater intimacy with God, 'the raising of the heart and mind to God',[14]; for God to open your spiritual eyes, and show you your soul in the midst of your heart.[15] Prayer and meditation give you that sense of belonging and a deep conviction that, regardless of what goes on around you, all will be well. The Pauline letters of scripture are full of such reassurances: 'Glory be to him whose power, working in us, can do infinitely more than we can ask or imagine' (Ephesians 3:20).

CHAPTER TWELVE

FAITH WITHOUT WORKS IS DEAD

Step Twelve: Having had a spiritual awakening as a result of these steps, we continued to practice these principles in all our affairs and carry the message to other alcoholics.

I don't think happiness or unhappiness is the point.
How do we meet the problems we face? How do we
best learn from them and transmit what we have
learned to others, if they would receive the knowledge?

In my view, we of this world are pupils in a great
school of life. It is intended that we try to grow, and
that we try to help our fellow travelers to grow in
the kind of love that makes no demands. In short,
we try to move toward the image and likeness of
God as we understand Him.

When pain comes, we are expected to learn from it
willingly, and help others to learn. When happiness
comes, we accept it as a gift, and thank God for it.
(Bill W, letter, 1950) [1]

GRAHAM'S STORY

For me Step Twelve has always been about freedom from the bondage of self through helping others. Sure, there is a certain amount of altruism involved but primarily when I am helping someone else it gets me out of myself. It gets back to what Socrates said on living the good life. He claimed that wisdom was knowledge because if everyone knew how good it made them feel and how beneficial it was for them when they helped others, everyone would do it. The biggest single problem confronting most people is egocentrism in varying degrees.

For me it is like an emotional chain and every time I do some form of service work it breaks another link in the chain. Anyone can do service work — a kind word when you're not in the mood, a smile at a passing stranger — it is all service work and aids and abets your spiritual wellbeing. I think the most important gift I can give anyone is my time. Sure, I can give someone food or money, or dispense some pithy wisdom, but to give up your time to someone — that is real service work. Going the extra distance, taking time out when there is nothing in it for me is a way I can do 'service' in the workplace and in any other area of my life.

～

KNOW YOURSELF, BE YOURSELF, FORGIVE YOURSELF, FORGET YOURSELF

One source of inspiration for the Twelve Step program in its early formation was the philosophy of 'faith without works is dead'. James' letter in the New Testament talks about this. Step Twelve has, as its underlying philosophy, that to truly have a spiritual awakening you need to take that spiritual awareness out into the world and help others. Graham's reflection shows that sometimes it is the simple act of being there for someone, giving them your time, that constitutes 'helping others'.

In practising these principles in all your affairs it is important to remember the three powerful forces that can lead you away from the spiritual life — power, prestige and possession. The goal is for things like money to become your servant, not your master. This means your spiritual condition takes precedence over your material condition. Freedom from fear is far more important than freedom from want.[2]

This Twelve Step journey is an awakening of your heart and mind to God and in Step Twelve you can see God around you in other people and feel the presence of the Spirit when you help others. No form of external reward could be substituted for:

> *Service, gladly rendered, obligations squarely met*
> *troubles well accepted or solved with God's help,*
> *the knowledge that at home or in the world*
> *outside we are partners in a common effort, the*
> *well-understood fact that in God's sight all human*
> *beings are important, the proof that love freely*
> *given surely brings a full return, the certainty that*
> *we are no longer isolated and alone in*
> *self-constructed prisons, the surety that we need*
> *no longer be square pegs in round holes but can fit*
> *and belong in God's scheme of things ...*
> *True ambition is not what we thought it was.*
> *True ambition is the desire to live usefully and*
> *walk humbly under the grace of God.*[3]

This process of self-knowledge combined with not being so self-centred and then helping others can be expressed as: 'know yourself, be yourself, forgive yourself and others, then forget yourself'. It is also a process that involves several key elements of the Christian spiritual tradition, a constant striving for detachment and a focus on connection.

In reconnecting with your real self, the 'unedited

version', and with God, you are in a position to go out and help others in whatever way you feel called to. It is important that this is done unconditionally in 'a love that makes no demands' way, as Bill W said. That way you know you are truly not out for personal gain or self-centred needs.

Many of the personal stories in this book have shown how such a way of being can lead to enhanced spiritual health and relief from states like depression. Bill W, a sufferer from bouts of depression, always recommended long walks and good deeds as a remedy for the malaise.

This journey of self-discovery may have also put you in touch with your own gifts, allowing you to be able to use them to enhance your own life and that of others. For example, you may have discovered you have an artistic bent and have found this a great avenue for self-expression. Someone else who is struggling within themselves may also realise that such an avenue can be therapeutic. This is all part of practising these principles leading to self-discovery and the Twelve Steps in all your affairs.

In the Old Testament the Israelites became lost and disconnected when they forgot their own story and when they forgot the debt they owed to God. You need to remember what you have come from in order to stay on your spiritual path and enrich your own and other people's lives. Connection to your own life story, understanding how it has influenced you, understanding what you have come from, and connection to a Higher Power allow you to open up to connect with others.

THOMAS MERTON: CONTEMPLATION IN A WORLD OF ACTION

The late Thomas Merton, a Trappist monk, was famous for his writing on contemplative prayer. After pursuing a literary career in New York, Merton converted to Catholicism and joined monastic life in the 1940s. Merton saw the difficulty in trying to live a spiritual, contemplative life in a world which focuses on the rational, the competitive, achievement and a 'winning is everything' philosophy. To be in the world but not of it, not to be dictated to by its illusions but being able to partake in it, is a challenge. How do you become open to embrace all of life, yet at the same time partake in an openness, emptiness and poverty of spirit as the mystics did?

Practising these principles in all your affairs may be as simple as taking your spiritual wisdom and contemplation into your own world of action and letting others see that there is something powerful within you that sustains you. An example of this might be not allowing yourself to be drawn into petty squabbles in a work situation, and keeping focused on your own tasks for that day. Having had a spiritual awakening as the result of these steps might mean being grateful for the fact that an addiction no longer controls you, for example, and seeing the way in which you were led to be free of that addiction.

Merton also stresses the importance of remaining connected to your own story, of owning your own experience and understanding how all of it has affected your life and seeing God's work in the pattern of your life:

> *Let us keep alive especially the awareness of what is really authentic within our own experience, because we know, we have experienced in moments of prayer, in moments of truth and realisation, what God really asks of us and what He really wishes to give us. Let us remain faithful to that truth and to that experience.*[4]

LOVING WITHOUT KNOWING

As you try to put this Step Twelve into your daily life, you need to integrate your spiritual experiences and your life experiences, both good and bad. To help others and change the society in which you live, you need to take with you self-knowledge, humility and charity. Most importantly you need to remind yourself, as the anonymous fourteenth – century author of *The Cloud of Unknowing* wrote, 'it is love alone that can reach God in this life, and not knowing'.[5]

HILDEGARD OF BINGEN:
A COSMIC FORCE OF HARMONY

Step Twelve is about integrating much of what you have learnt along the way in your spiritual journey. It is a holistic program. The mystics offered excellent examples of integrated consciousness as they went about their lives. For example, Mechthild taught that desire for God is your greatest treasure.[6] Teresa of Avila showed that Jesus or God is your friend. Julian of Norwich found that Jesus is also your mother:

And then will the bliss of our motherhood in Christ
be to begin anew in the joys of our Father, God,
which new beginnings will last, newly beginning
without end. [7]

The Benedictine Hildegard of Bingen, a popular figure at the turn of the twelfth century, put forward a holistic spirituality that was cosmic and unique in its femininity and comprehension of human nature. 'Tithing' was not an uncommon practice in medieval Europe, and as the tenth child of a noble family, Hildegard was placed in the care of a recluse, Jutta, in a nearby religious community. Jutta later founded a Benedictine convent and Hildegard became a Benedictine nun at the age of eighteen. Hildegard had supernatural visions from a young age and when she became abbess of the Benedictine community in 1136 she began recording some of her visionary experiences. Even a commission by the pope of the day proclaimed her visions to be of genuine divine inspiration. She was not only a mystic, but a musician, poet, artist, and what we might class as a naturopath. She was a friend and advisor to kings, queens and monastics, and a woman who sought to reform her church. This influential woman understood there was a cosmic force of unity operating in the universe:

O most steadfast path,
Which penetrates all things:
in the highest places, on the plains,
And in every abyss,
You summon and unite all. [8]

What makes Hildegard unique in late medieval society is that her writings and visions captured a cosmic, inter-connected holistic approach to life, while still espousing the Benedictine values of unity, balance, harmony and stability. This unique cosmic, creation-centred view of theology and humankind reflected the cycles of life, valued the feminine and did not shy away from the blend of the divine and the human.

Hildegard's writings also reflected the mood of Christian Renaissance humanism that was prevalent at the time, where knowledge and faith were held in high esteem, and spirituality was deeply affected by the personal and the human. Love and the soul's yearning for intercourse with the divine were emphasised, as was the positive nature of the human being.

Described as Benedictine to the core and embodying poverty of spirit, Hildegard always paid homage to the glory of God and stressed that only the humble possess true vision. Her mystical path of asceticism and detachment, prayer and contemplation, allowed for periods of spiritual dryness through purification in order to emerge with true humility and a right relationship between self and God. This and her emphasis on the humanity of Christ make her a source of wisdom and inspiration for us today.

As you carry your spiritual message to others, in whatever way you can, you hope that this serenity may touch other people and open them up to the possibility of change in their own life. As Hildegard writes in the illumination of her first vision, your potential is to 'come to light in the knowledge of mysteries ... where with a bright light this serenity will shine forth strongly among those who shine forth'.[9]

CONCLUSION
THE JOURNEY OF FREEDOM

This journey of freedom with the Twelve Steps and the Christian spiritual and mystical tradition started with the admission of powerlessness. It is an uncertain journey bringing freedom from bondage.

The Twelve Step movement, which began when two human beings suffering the same burden helped each other, tapped into great truths about the human condition. As Swiss psychiatrist Paul Tournier said when describing the Oxford Group, it may well have done what the church was failing to do at that time, 'to find out what was happening in people's souls ... There is still too much talking, but silence has returned. Frank [Buchman, the founder of the Oxford movement] helped to show again that the power of silence is the power of God.'[1]

BEDE GRIFFITHS: YOU ARE PART OF A NEW CREATION

We are passing into a new age. However, as Bill W said, we do not know what form this new era will take.

Bede Griffiths speaks of a reconnection, of a force that is transforming humanity. All over the world, despite the existence of much turmoil and suffering, more and more people are turning to a spiritual path, 'bringing everything into the inner centre of the heart and finding the meaning of life, not in the external world but in the inner reality ...'[2] Many are seeking what the Jesuit Karl Rahner described as 'the holy mystery', the mystery behind everything.

These Twelve Steps, like the paths of the great mystics, may involve trying to let go of things that hold you back from God. The spiritual life can sometimes be painful, but it is always mysterious and ultimately fulfilling. As Mechthild reminds us:

> God leads his chosen children
> Along strange paths
> And it is a strange path
> And a noble path,
> Which God himself walked...[3]

The ultimate result of letting go is to respond to the Spirit working in the world, so a new age will dawn. For 'our human nature is called to be one with God. There is no other way.'[4]

You are asking yourself, as all of us must:
'Who am I?'...'where am I?'...'Whence do I go?'
The process of enlightenment is usually slow.
But, in the end, our seeking always brings a finding.
These great mysteries are, after all,
enshrined in complete simplicity.

(Bill W)[5]

ENDNOTES

EPIGRAPH
1. Dante, The Divine Comedy, Hell, p. 71.

INTRODUCTION
1. Bede Griffiths, *The New Creation in Christ*, Darton, Longman and Todd, London, 1992, p. 76.
2. Garth Lean, *Frank Buchman: A Life*, Constable and Company Ltd, Great Britain, 1985, p. 31.
3. *Pass it On, The story of Bill Wilson and how the AA message reached the world*, Alcoholics Anonymous World Services Inc, New York, 1984, p. 127.
4. Bill W, 'Alcoholics Anonymous Beginnings and Growth', talk presented to the New York City Medical Society on Alcoholism, 28 April 1958. In *'Three Talks to Medical Societies by Bill W, co-founder of AA'*, Alcoholics Anonymous World Services Inc, New York, p. 10.
5. ibid., p. 12.
6. *The Best of Bill, from the Grapevine*, The AA Grapevine Inc, 1990, p. 15.
7. ibid., p. 16.
8. Alcoholics Anonymous: *The Big Book*, 3rd edn, Alcoholics Anonymous World Services Inc, New York, 1976, pp. 59–60.
9. ibid., p. 17.
10. Gerald May, 'Love and Spirituality in the Healing of Addiction', *Addiction and Grace*, Harper, San Francisco, 1988, p. 1.
11. Carl Jung, ed. Aniela Jaffe, *Memories, Dreams and Reflections*, Collins, Great Britain, 1963, p. 17.
12. Robert Thomsen, *Bill W*, Hamish Hamilton, London, 1976, p. 363.
13. Demetrius Dumm, *Flowers in the Desert*, Paulist Press, Mahwah, New Jersey, 1987, p. 106.
14. See quotes defining 'mystic' in *The World Treasury of*

Religious Quotations, Garland Books, New York, 1966, p. 664.

15. For further explanation of what constitutes a mystic, see FC Happold, *Mysticism, A Study and an Anthology*, Penguin, London, 1970, esp. pp. 35–37, 45–47.

16. *Alcoholics Anonymous*, p. 60.

CHAPTER 1

1. 'Alcoholics Anonymous – beginnings and growth', Presented to the New York City Medical Society on Alcoholism, 28 April, 1958, p. 14.

2. Morgan Costelloe, 1997, 'The Spirituality of Matt Talbot', *Spirituality*, Dublin 12:178.

3. Demetrius Dumm, 1987, *Flowers in the Desert*, Paulist Press, New York, p. 5.

4. See Paul Tillich's ideas on 'New Being as Process', *Systematic Theology*, 1973, vol. 3, University of Chicago Press, p. 53.

5. *Alcoholics Anonymous: The Big Book*, 3rd edn., 1976, Alcoholics Anonymous World Services Inc, New York, p. 60.

6. Victor Frankl, 1984, *Man's Search for Meaning*, Washington Square Press, New York, p. 121.

7. Dumm, p. 6.

8. ibid., p. 5.

9. Origen, 'First Homily on the Song of Songs', in Ancient Christian Writers, 1957, trans. R.P. Lawson, Newman, New York, no. 26, p. 491.

10. Origen, 'Homily XXVII on Numbers, 4,' in *Origen, An Exhortation to Martyrdom, Prayer & Selected Works*, 1979, trans. Rowan A Greer, Paulist Press, New York, pp 250–251.

11. John of the Cross, 'The Dark Night', Prologue, in *The Collected Works of John of the Cross*, trans. Kieran Kavanaugh and Otilio Rodriguez, 1973, ICS Publications, Washington, DC, p. 295.

12. John of the Cross, *The Ascent of Mount Carmel*, I:1-2;13 in ibid., pp 74–75; 101–104.

13. See Iain Matthew, 1995, *The Impact of God*, Hodder & Stoughton, London, p. 26.

14. John of the Cross, 'Ascent of Mount Carmel', 2:4.5, *The Collected Works of John of the Cross*, p. 114.

15. John of the Cross, letter 33, to a Carmelite nun, late 1591, in Iain Matthew, *The Impact of God*, p. 131.

CHAPTER 2

1. *Bill W,* presented to the New York City Medical Society on Alcoholism, 28 April 1958.

2. 'This Matter of Fear', from *The Best of Bill*, p. 15.

3. *Alcoholics Anonymous*, p. 60.

4. Morris West, *Lazarus*, quoted in A View from the Ridge, Harper, San Francisco, 1994, p. 135.

5. Robert Thomsen, *Bill W*, Hamish Hamilton, London, 1975, p. 363.

6. Jung, *Memories, Dreams and Reflections*, p. 373.

7. Joseph A Fitzmyer, *The New Jerome Biblical Commentry*, Geoffrey Chapman, New York, 1990, pp. 82:78, 1401.

8. J Behm, 'Metamorphoo', *Theological Dictionary of the New Testament*, vol. 4, p. 757.

CHAPTER 3

1. The Spiritual Exercises of St Ignatius, 'St Ignatius' Prayer, no. 234'.

2. *Twelve Steps and Twelve Traditions*, Alcoholics Anonymous World Services Inc, New York, 1978, p. 36.

3. *Alcoholics Anonymous*, p. 63.

4. Benedicta Ward, *The Sayings of the Desert Fathers*, Mowbrays, London and oxford, 1975, pp. 6–7.

5. Rufinus' prologue to *Historia Monachorum in Aegypto*, in ibid., p. 50.

6. *Alcoholics Anonymous*, p. 164.

7. Timothy Fry, ed., *The Rule of St Benedict in English*, Liturgical Press, Minnesota, 1982, pp. 15–16.

8. *Alcoholics Anonymous*, p. 58.

Chapter 4

1. Extract from *The Gospel of St Thomas*, no. 70, Nag Hammadi Library.
2. Alcoholics Anonymous, p. 71.
3. ibid., p. 68.
4. Lewis Delmage, trans., *The Spiritual Exercises of St Ignatius Loyola*, St Paul Editions, Boston, 1978, no. 4, p. 20.
5. ibid., no. 1, p. 19.
6. ibid., no. 43, p. 38.
7. ibid., no. 44, p. 39.
8. ibid., nos. 316, 317, p. 155.
9. ibid., no. 319, p. 156.
10. ibid., no. 186, p. 99.
11. Kieran Kavanaugh & Otilio Rodriquez, trans., 'The Ascent of Mount Carmel', in *The collected works of St John of the Cross*, ICS Publications, Washington DC, 1973, 1:13, pp. 11, 104.
12. John Cassian Conferences 9, Paulist Press, New York, 1985.

Chapter 5

1. Extract from The Gospel of St Thomas, no. 5, Nag Hammadi Library
2. Iain Matthew, *The Impact of God*, Hodder & Stoughton, London, 1995, pp. 24–25.
3. *Twelve Steps and Twelve Traditions*, p. 125.
4. Robert J Miller, ed., *The Gospel of Thomas*, no. 3, in *The Complete Gospels*, Harper, San Francisco, Sonoma, 1972, p. 305.
5. *Daily Reflections*, Alcoholics Anonymous World Services Inc, New York, p. 107.
6. Matthew, 'The Ascent of Mt Carmel' 2A 17.3, Canticle B 23.6, 'The Living Flame of Love' LF 3.59, p. 15.
7. *Alcoholics Anonymous*, p. 68.
8. ibid., p. 60.

9. Matthew, 'Ascent of Mt Carmel, 1A 9.1, p. 15.

10. *Twelve Steps and Twelve Traditions*, p. 59.

11. ibid., p. 58.

12. Benedicta Ward, *The Lives of the Desert Fathers*, Cistercian Publications, Michigan, 1980, p. 33.

13. Fry, ed., 1, 15, Prologue, The Rule of St Benedict in English.

14. Main, *The Christian Mysteries*, Prayer and Sacrament, The Benedictine Priory of Montreal, Canada, 1979, p. 50.

15. David L Fleming SJ, ed., *The Spiritual Exercises of St Ignatius, A Literal Translation and a Contemporary Reading*, trans. Elder Mullan SJ, Institute of Jesuit Sources, Missouri, 1978, nos. 36–37, 53–54.

16. *Alcoholics Anonymous*, p. 69.

17. Fleming & SJ, ed., no. 176, pp. 106–107.

18. ibid., no. 135, p. 84.

19. ibid., no. 135, p. 85.

20. ibid., nos. 136–146, pp. 86–89.

21. ibid., no. 327, pp. 216–217.

22. C Luibheid, ed., John Cassian Conferences, CWS Series, New York, 1985, 9.15.

23. ibid., 9.27.

24. Happold, pp. 237–238.

25. Julian of Norwich, 'Showings', 258, quoted in Carol Lee Flinders, ed., *A Little Book of Women Mystics*, Harper, San Francisco, 1995, p. 47.

CHAPTER 6

1. The Rule of Benedict, 20.3, p. 48

2. *As Bill Sees It*, Alcoholics Anonymous World Services Inc, New York, p. 115.

3. Richard Rohr, OFM, speaking at a seminar entitled 'Male Spirituality', in Aquinas Academy, Sydney, November 2000.

4. Fleming & SJ, ed., no. 46, p. 32.

5. ibid., nos. 314–318, pp. 208–210.

6. See a contemporary reading of ibid., nos. 313–336, p. 206.

7. ibid., no. 315, p. 208.

8. ibid., no. 195, p. 118.

CHAPTER 7

1. St Augustine, Confessions, VIII, 7, p. 169

2. *Twelve Steps and Twelve Traditions*, p. 75.

3. *Alcoholics Anonymous*, p. 76.

4. John Main, 'Christian Meditation', The Gethsemani Talks, X, Christian Meditation Media, Canada, 1982, 19.

5. Fleming SJ, ed., 'The Three Types of People', nos. 152–155, 92–95.

6. ibid., III, pp. 9, 67.

7. ibid., VI, pp. 1, 111.

8. ibid., VIII, pp. 11, 175.

9. ibid., VIII, pp. 12, 177.

10. ibid., X, pp. 26, 231.

11. ibid., X, pp. 32, 238.

12. ibid., VIII, pp. 11, 176.

CHAPTER 8

1. *Alcoholics Anonymous*, p. 83.

CHAPTER 9

1. The Rule of Benedict, Prologue, no. 35

2. Fleming SJ, ed., nos. 24–47, pp. 24–33.

3. ibid., nos. 189, 240, p. 114–?, 144–145.

4. ibid., no. 82, pp. 54–55.

5. Main, *The Christian Mysteries*, p. 50.

6. ibid., p. 47.

7. Rohr, 'Male Spirituality'.

8. Main, *The Christian Mysteries*, p. 51.

9. Abba Pachomius in Ward, p. 45.

10. Fry, ed., pp. 35–38, 18.

11. Bill W, letter, in *As Bill Sees It*, p. 168.

CHAPTER 10

1. *Alcoholics Anonymous*, p. 84.
2. *Twelve Steps and Twelve Traditions*, p. 95.
3. Fleming & SJ, ed., nos. 314, 315, 317–321, pp. 208–213.
4. ibid., nos. 324, 326, 327, p. 214–217.
5. Main, *The Christian Mysteries*, p. 47.
6. Julian of Norwich, 'Showings' (Short Text), in Monica Furlong, *Visions and Longings*, Mowbrays, London, 1950, p. 191.
7. Julian of Norwich, 'Showings' (Long Text), in ibid., p. 241.
8. Julian of Norwich, 'Showings', in *Revelations of Divine Love*, Penguin, London, p. 35.
9. Julian of Norwich, 'Showings' (Short Text), in Furlong, p. 213.

CHAPTER 11

1. Jose de Vinck, ed., Mechthild of Magdeburg, VII: 56, in *Revelations of Women Mystics from Middle Ages to Modern Times*, Alleluia Press, New York, 1985, pp. 5–7, 12–23.
2. Theresa of Avila, *Collected Works*, 8.5, quoted in Flinders, p. 88.
3. Thanks to the nuns at the Benedictine Abbey, Jamberoo, New South Wales, for their weekend lectures on *lectio divina*.
4. Fleming & SJ, ed., nos. 232–234, pp. 138–140.
5. ibid., no. 234, p. 140.
6. ibid., no. 233, p. 138.
7. ibid., no. 330, pp. 218–219.
8. ibid., no. 231, p. 138.
9. Julian of Norwich, 'Showings' (Short Text), in Furlong, p. 192.
10. ibid., p. 194.
11. ibid., p. 195.
12. ibid., pp. 204–205.
13. ibid., pp. 225–226.
14. *Twelve Steps and Twelve Traditions*, p. 102.

15. Julian of Norwich, 'Showings' (Short Text), in Furlong, p. 228.

CHAPTER 12
1. *As Bill Sees It*, p. 306.
2. *Twelve Steps and Twelve Traditions*, p. 122
3. ibid., pp. 124–125.
4. Thomas Merton, *Contemplation in a World of Action*, Unwin Paperbacks, London, 1980, p. 355.
5. *The Cloud of Unknowing*, 44, in Henry C Simmons, ed., *In the Footsteps of the Mystics*, Paulist Press, NJ, 1992, pp. 138–139.
6. See the dialogue between the Soul and God in 'The Love Chase', in de Vinck, ed., 1:39–43, pp. 5–7, 12–23.
7. Julian of Norwich, 'Showings' (Long Text), in Furlong, p. 246. See also pp. 236, 238.
8. Hildegard of Bingen, *De Spiritu Sancto* (To the Holy Spirit), in 'Songs' in *Book of Divine Works*, Bear & Company, Santa Fe, New Mexico, 1987, p. 373.
9. Hildegard of Bingen, 'Scivias', p. 8, quoted in Matthew Fox, ed., *Illuminations of Hildegard of Bingen*, Bear & Company, Santa Fe, 1985, p. 9.

CONCLUSION
1. Lean, p. 153.
2. Griffiths, p. 71.
3. Mechtild of Magdeburg, 'On the Way of Suffering for God Joyfully', in Furlong, p. 114.
4. Griffiths, p. 81.
5. Bill W, letter, in Came to Believe, 1973, Alcoholics Anonymous World Services, Inc, New York, p. 53.

The author and the publishers would like to acknowledge the kind of permission given by the following sources to reproduce material. Every effort has been made to contact all holders of copyright material included in *Steps to Life*.

The Best of Bill W, published by *The Grapevine*, quotes are reprinted with permission from The AA Grapevine Inc, New York.

The Collected Works of St John of the Cross, translated by Kieran Kavanaugh and Otilio Rodriguez. Excerpts reprinted with the permission of ICS Publications/Spiritual Life, 2131 Lincoln Rd, NE Washington DC 20002-1199, USA, www.icspublications.org

Confessions, by St Augustine, translated by RS Pine-Coffin. Excerpts reprinted with the permission of The Penguin Group, London.

Flowers in the Desert, by Demetrius Dumm. Excerpts reprinted with the permission of Paulist Press Inc, New York/Mahwah NJ.

Frank Buchman: A Life, by Garth Lean. Excerpts reprinted with the permission of Alisa Hamilton, Constable and Company, London.

'The Gospel of Thomas' in *The Complete Gospels*, edited by Robert J Miller. Excerpts reprinted with permission of HarperCollins Publishers, Sonoma.

John Cassian Conferences in CWS Series, edited by C Luibheid. Excerpts reprinted with the permission of Paulist Press Inc, New York/Mahwah NJ.

Mysticism, A Study and an Anthology, by FC Happold.

Excerpts reprinted with the permission of The Penguin Group, London.

The New Creation in Christ, by Bede Griffiths. Excerpts reprinted with the permission of Darton, Longman and Todd Ltd, London.

Origen, An Exhortation to Martyrdom, Prayer and Selected Works, translated by Rowan A Greer. Excerpts reprinted with the permission of Paulist Press Inc, New York/Mahwah NJ.

Revelations of Divine Love, by Julian of Norwich, translated by Elizabeth Spearing. Excerpts reprinted with the permission of The Penguin Group, London.

The Rule of St Benedict in English, edited by Timothy Fry. Excerpts reprinted with the permission of Liturgical Press, Philadelphia.

The Sayings of the Desert Fathers, by Benedicta Ward, translated by Norman Russell. Excerpts reprinted with the permission of Cistercian Publications.

Sister of Wisdom, St Hildegard's Theology of the Feminine, by Barbara Newman. Excerpts reprinted with the permission of The Regents of the University of California.

A View From The Ridge, by Morris West. Excerpts reprinted with the permission of HarperCollins Publishers, New York and San Francisco.

BIBLIOGRAPHY

Alcoholics Anonymous, 1976, Alcoholics Anonymous World Services Inc, New York.

As Bill Sees It, 1967, Alcoholics Anonymous World Services Inc, New York.

Augustine of Hippo, *Selected Writings*, 1984, translated by Mary T Clark, Paulist Press, New York.

'Alcoholics Anonymous Beginnings and Growth', Bill W talk presented to the New York City Medical Society on Alcoholism, 28 April 1958, in *'Three talks to Medical Societies' by Bill W*, co-founder of AA, Alcoholics Anonymous World Services Inc, New York.

'Basic concepts of Alcoholics Anonymous', excerpts from an address presented by Bill W to the Medical Society of the State of New York. Section on Neurology and Psychiatry Annual Meeting, New York, NY, May 1944, in *'Three talks to Medical Societies' by Bill W, co-founder of AA*. Alcoholics Anonymous World Services Inc, New York.

Boulding, Maria OSB, 'St Benedict of Nursia'.

Bowie, Fiona, 1989, *Beguine Spirituality, An Anthology*, translated by Oliver Davies, SPCK, London.

Bowie, F and Davies, O, ed., 1990, 'Scivias', in *Hildegard of Bingen. An Anthology*, SPCK, London.

Brundell, Michael, 'Discovering the Diamond, Signposts for the Inner Journey: The Interior Castle of Saint Teresa of Avila', in *Spirituality*, vol. 2, no. 6, May – June 1996.

Came to Believe, 1973, Alcoholics Anonymous World Services Inc, New York.

Cameron, Peter John, 1996, *The Classics of Catholic Spirituality*, Alba House, New York.

Capps, WH, and Wright, WM, ed., 1978, *Silent Fire. An Invitation to Western Mysticism*. New York.

Cassian, John *Conference 10. The Second conference of the Abbot Isaac on Prayer.*

The Collected Works of John of the Cross, translated by Kieran Kavanaugh and Otilio Rodriguez, 1973, ICS Publications, Washington.

Costelloe, Morgan, 'The Spirituality of Matt Talbot', in *Spirituality* vol. 12, 1997.

Daily Reflections, 1990, Alcoholics Anonymous World Services Inc, New York.

Delmage, Lewis SJ, ed. 1978, *The Spiritual Exercises of St. Ignatius Loyola*, St Paul editions, Philadelphia.

Dumm, Demetrius, *Flowers in the Desert*, 1987, Paulist Press, Mahwah, NJ.

De Waal, Esther, 1996, *Seeking God: The Way of St Benedict*, Fount, London.

Fleming, David L, ed. 1978, *The Spiritual Exercises of St Ignatius, A Literal Translation and a Contemporary Reading*, translated by Elder Mullan SJ, India: Gujarat Sahitya Prakash Anand, in cooperation with The Institute of Jesuit Sources, Missouri.

Flinders, Carol Lee ed., 1995, *A Little Book of Women Mystics*, Harper, San Francisco.

Fox, Matthew ed., 1987, *Hildegard of Bingen's Book of Divine Works I*, Bear & Company, Santa Fe, New Mexico.

Fox, Matthew, 1987, *Illuminations of Hildegard of Bingen*, Bear & Company, Santa Fe, New Mexico.

Francis of Assisi, *The Writings*, in *Classics of Western Spirituality*, translated by RJ Armstrong and IC Brady, 'The Canticle of Brother Sun.'

Frankl, Victor, 1984, *Man's Search for Meaning*, Washington Square Press, New York.

Fry, Timothy, ed. 1982, *The Rule of St. Benedict in English*, Liturgical Press, Minnesota.

Furlong, Monica, 1950, *Visions and Longings*, Mowbrays, London.

Griffiths, Bede, 1992, *The New Creation in Christ*, Darton, Longmann & Todd, London.

Happold, FC, ed., 1970, *Mysticism, A Study and An Anthology*, Pelican Books, London.

Jager, Willigis, 1995, *Search for the Meaning of Life. Essays and Reflections on the Mystical Experience*, Triumph, Missouri.

Jung, Carl, (Aniela Jaffe, ed.), 1963, *Memories, Dreams and Reflections*, Collins, Great Britain.

Lean, Garth, 1985, *Frank Buchman: A Life*, Constable and Company Ltd, London.

McGinn, Bernard and Meyendorff, Jean Leclercq, ed., 1985, *Christian Spirituality*, Crossroad, New York.

Luibheid, C, ed., 1985, *John Cassian Conferences*, CSW Series, New York.

Main, Dom John, 1979, *Christian Mysteries, Prayer and Sacrament*, The Benedictine Priory of Montreal, Canada.

Main, Dom John, 1982, *Christian Meditation, The Gethsemani Talks*, Christian Meditation Media, Canada.

Matthews, Iain, 1995, *The Impact of God*, Hodder & Stoughton, London.

May, Gerald, 1988, *Addiction and Grace*, HarperCollins, San Francisco.

Merton, Thomas, 1980, *Contemplation in a World of Action*, Unwin Paperbacks, London.

Miller, Robert J, ed. 1992, *The Gospel of Thomas in The Complete Gospels*, Harper, San Francisco, Sonoma.

Newman, Barbara, 1987, *Sister of Wisdom, St Hildegard's Theology of the Feminine*, University of California Press, Los Angeles.

Origen, An Exhortation to Martyrdom, Prayer & Selected Works, 1979, translated by Rowan A Greer, Paulist Press, New York.

Rahner, Karl, *Mission and Grace*, vol. 3.

Rohr, Richard, taped lecture, 2000, 'Male Spirituality', Aquinas Academy, Sydney.

Saint Augustine, *Confessions*, translated by RS Pine-Coffin, 1961, Penguin, Middlesex.

Simmons, Henry C, 1992, *In the Footsteps of the Mystics*, Paulist Press, New Jersey.

Tarnas, Richard, 1991, *The Passion of the Western Mind*, Pimlico, London.

'This matter of fear', *The Best of Bill, from the Grapevine*, 1990, The AA Grapevine Inc, New York.

Thomsen, Robert , 1975, *Bill W*, Hamish Hamilton, London.

Tillich, Paul, 1963, *Systematic Theology*, vol. 3, University of Chicago Press.

Twelve Steps and Twelve Traditions, 1952, Alcoholics Anonymous World Services Inc., New York.

de Vinck, Jose, ed., 1985, *Revelations of Women Mystics from Middle Ages to Modern Times*, New York.

Ward, Benedicta, 1975, *The Sayings of the Desert Fathers*, translated by Benedicta Ward, Mowbrays, London and Oxford.

Ward, Benedicta, 1980, *The Lives of the Desert Fathers*, translated by Norman Russell, Cistercian Publications, Michigan.

West, Morris, 1994, *A View From A Ridge*, Harper, San Francisco.